Changing the World...
10 Seconds at a Time

Alyssa,

U-Matter!

Bobby Petrocelli

10seconds.org

To contact Bobby Petrocelli for
appearance or booking
information, please contact us on
our website at:

10seconds.org or bobbypetrocelli.com

or write:

10 Seconds
PO Box 3396
Seminole, FL 33775

For other books, information or product offered by
10 Seconds, please contact us on our website at:

10seconds.org

10 SECONDS

will
~~can~~ change your life
Forever

BOBBY PETROCELLI

HONOR NET
THE HONOR NETWORK

10 Seconds Can Change Your Life Forever
Copyright © 2005 by Bobby Petrocelli

ISBN # 0-9753036-2-7

Published by:
 HonorNet
 P.O. Box 910
 Sapulpa, OK 74067

Fifth printing, September 2008

Dedication

Suzy, Alec, and Aron...
*For your immeasurable support and
allowing me to do what I love to do*

To All My Family and Friends...
For being there when I need you the most and not having to be asked

To the Hurting of the World...
That you may find hope, faith, and love

In Loving Memory of...

Ava Lynn Dorsett Petrocelli

TABLE OF
CONTENTS

Suzy's Message ix
A Thankful Heart xi
Foreword xiii
Prologue: Am I Dreaming? xv
Chapter 1: Boy from Brooklyn 1
Chapter 2: College Days 17
Chapter 3: Texas Belle 35
Chapter 4: Full of Dreams 47
Chapter 5: Thursday, October 24, 1985 61
Chapter 6: Rude Awakening 73
Chapter 7: The Truth Hurts 81
Chapter 8: Reality TV 87
Chapter 9: Reality TV Too 95
Chapter 10: 10 Seconds 101

Chapter 11: Can I Ever Live Again? 109
Chapter 12: Beginning to See the Light 119
Chapter 13: Give Faith a Fighting Chance 125
Chapter 14: Forgiveness Is Optional. 131
Chapter 15: Family and Friends 137
Chapter 16: Growth Is Optional. 145
Chapter 17: Hope Is a Good Thing. 151
Chapter 18: Can I Love Again?. 157
Chapter 19: It's Always Something—Par for the Course. 173
Chapter 20: Can I Make a Difference? 179
Chapter 21: Youth Nation 183
Chapter 22: When It's All Been Said and Done 195
Appendix: Quotes to Live By 203
About the Author 205

SUZY'S MESSAGE

God has given my husband a very special gift; the gift to connect to people, feel their pain, and be truly genuine. Bobby has a heart to see people succeed. He is doing what he does best. He is an encourager—encouraging others to reach their fullest potential. Through sharing his own experiences of the joys and sorrows that make up life, he offers inspiration that hearts can be restored, despair can be turned to hope, and sorrow can become joy.

I support him in sharing his message. Yes, it's difficult, when he travels and is gone from home. But in the end, when we get thousands of e-mails from people saying how his message changed their lives, what can you say? It's all about touching hearts and changing lives for the better. You have to look at the big picture. It's easy to focus on yourself, but when you focus outward, things like that don't seem to matter as much.

Sometimes it's difficult to believe that Bobby even experienced such a horrific ordeal, because he lives each day to its fullest. Life is priceless; therefore, he tries to communicate to others how significant all decisions are.

Bobby Petrocelli is a man of courage, fervor, and immovable faith. He is a solid pillar of strength. As a husband and father, he shows this strength in every aspect of his life. He may get up in front of an audience by himself, but when he shares, both of us are really up there. (All his good points are my ideas anyway!) I love him, admire him, and will treasure him always.

Suzy Petrocelli

A
THANKFUL
HEART

More than ever, I recognize the importance of relationships in our lives. I received so much support through prayers, letters, flowers, visitations, and phone calls—an outpouring of the love of so many. It would take more pages than there are in this book to thank everybody. Let me summarize by saying this:

Suzy, I am truly the most blessed man in the world to have such an incredible wife. Alec and Aron, you are the greatest sons a dad could ever ask for. To every awesome friend and family member, you are simply the best. Cheeks and Jake, thanks for being a major part of this project. The list goes on and on.

Most of all, I thank You, God. "Without You I can do nothing." You have shown me what a privileged man I am.

If you were there for me in any way, your efforts have not gone unnoticed. Thank you, thank you, thank you. The best part of it all is, **We are changing the world…10 Seconds at a time!!**

FOREWORD

In a time when much of our world is in turmoil and most of the news is anything but good, Bobby's inspiring story of faith, courage, and love will touch your heart and provide a reminder that no matter how lonely, how dark, how difficult circumstances may seem, we, too, can triumph over anything that might stand in our way.

He's a real-life "Rocky," and his story is a knockout!

Every young person in America should read this book so that they will know—without a doubt—the irreversible dangers of drinking and driving and the unequaled importance of making responsible choices. And by the same token, every parent and adult should also read this book so that they, too, will understand how critical it is to establish a strong foundation of responsibility in our youth.

Each of us can make a difference, but we each have to take the first step.

Bobby Petrocelli's life is now dedicated to bringing hope to all who will listen. He's an example to all of us that we, too, can live victorious and triumphant lives.

Ann Jillian
Actress

PROLOGUE

Am I
Dreaming?

THURSDAY, OCTOBER 24, 1985. LEAGUE CITY, TEXAS.

My wife, Ava, left that morning to go to work in Pasadena, Texas, a city south of Houston, where she worked in the offices of a concrete plant. I left for my job in nearby Alta Loma, where I taught health education and coached at Santa Fe High School. Baseball and track I didn't mind so much, but the hours I put in during football season were long and grueling: seven days a week, August through November. In Texas, they live and breathe high-school football. For me, it was my job, but for these Texans, football was their life.

I got home about 10:30 that night, which was normal during the season. Two of my greatest loves were waiting for me: my beloved wife, Ava, and a Jethro-Bodine-sized bowl of rigatoni. What more out of life do Italian men want than a loving wife and a jumbo bowl of pasta? Well, throw in *The Honeymooners*, a second helping of pasta with homemade sauce, a few hours of sleep, and I'm rejuvenated for another day. Another day. Tomorrow. The sun always comes up tomorrow, right?

Of course.

After dinner, Ava and I settled down in the living room, where she nestled into my lap to talk about the day's events and what was coming up with the approach of the holidays. Each night, when I came home from practice, I anticipated holding Ava like this in my lap. It was such a simple pleasure, having my baby cuddle up to me each night and softly talking about her day.

One of the greatest feelings of being married is the intimacy, especially the kind of intimacy I had with Ava. It's funny to see big, hulking men melt like butter in the presence of the woman they love. I saw it in the other coaches, and I saw it in myself—when our loves were nearby, we melted like ice cream on the sidewalk on a hot July afternoon.

Ava and I had moved into a new house two months earlier, around Labor Day. It was a fresh start, with no more small apartments and no more small rooms. After two-and-a-half years of marriage, we were finally settling into the life we wanted. We couldn't have been happier.

I was still wound up from the long day when we said goodnight and went to bed at 11:30. I tossed and turned for five minutes before getting up and stumbling my way through the dark into the kitchen for a glass of milk. When I opened the refrigerator door, I was disappointed to see that there was none. Milk always calmed me down and helped me sleep, but instead, I had a glass of water. I went back to bed and asked Ava about the milk situation, and she mumbled she would get a fresh gallon in the morning. She was a good wife. She knew what I liked, and I liked cereal, juice, and toast in the morning. I couldn't have asked for a better mate. I kissed her cheek good-night, and we both fell asleep.

About an hour later, I woke up. But instead of being in my bed, I was sitting in my dining-room window—one room away. I was confused. I was dazed. The smell of sulfur, tar, and burning rubber filled the room. Sulfur? Tar? Burning rubber? This dream was *vivid*. There was a stench about it, an unmistakable stench. I dropped my head for a moment, then picked it up and saw flickering lights coming through a foggy haze. Lights? Haze? The smell of tar and burning rubber grew stronger.

What a weird dream. What a weird feeling. I kept waiting to wake up. Somebody—wake me up.

I dropped my head a second time. When I looked up, there was a pickup truck directly in front of me. The smell. The stench. The lights. The truck.

A third time I dropped my head. Then I looked up quickly once again, trying desperately to shake myself out of this funk—this stupor I was in. Blue. The truck was blue and white. My bed was gone, and there was a blue and white pickup truck in my house. I saw a man step out of the truck. He looked at me, and I stared back at him. After an awkward moment of silence, he said to me, "Is there anyone else in the house?"

What? Who is this man? What's this truck doing in my house?

"Is there somebody else in this house?"

I was silent as my brain went numb. Is there somebody else in the house? *Is there somebody else in the house?*

My wife. My wife! Where is my wife?

CHAPTER 1

Boy from Brooklyn

Beepa shook me again, this time harder. "Time to get up," he said in his thick Swedish accent. "Bobby, it's *time* to get up."

My older sister, Debbie, and I used to mimic Nanny and Beepa's accent all the time. It was both funny and foreign to us. Beepa was from Sweden and Nanny was from Norway. They were our grandparents on my mother's side. My grandmother's real name was Gunhilde, and my grandfather's name was August Torsten. Gunhilde and August Torsten Carlson. To us, they were simply Nanny and Beepa. It was much easier that way.

Beepa had heard me screaming and rushed into the room to wake me up. "You ver screaming, Bobby. Are you all right now?" he asked with loving concern in his voice.

"Yes, Beepa. Where am I?"

Beepa hugged me. "You're at our house in de mountains, of course. Vhere did you think you ver? Don't you remember ve vent fishing today?" I sat in a sleepy stupor for a moment. I blinked my eyes and tried to shake the cobwebs out of my head. I was confused. This nightmare seemed real. It lingered vividly. Just then Nanny rushed into the room with a wet washcloth and a cold glass of water. No sooner had she stepped into the room than Beepa shot a sharp remark at her in Norwegian. Nanny snapped back as quick as a pistol. I didn't catch everything they said, but I knew it was about the spicy food I had had for dinner. Beepa made another biting comment, and Nanny hit him with the washcloth on the shoulder. This was how they squabbled. Nanny carried a mean washcloth. It was loaded and ready for another strike.

Beepa got wise and didn't say another word. "Ve're here, Bobby," Nanny said. "You're safe vith us now." Debbie stormed into the room and said, "It's *time* to get up," in Nanny and Beepa's accent. She could always make me laugh. I looked outside and saw it was still dark. The lightning bugs flickered beautifully in the night. Their lights flicked on, then off, in the blackened night. I breathed in deeply and filled my lungs with the crisp mountain air. I looked out into the darkness and did it again. "What're you doin'?" Debbie asked, puzzled.

Deep breath in. Release.

"What're you doin'?" Debbie asked again in a more critical tone. "Beepa got gas again?" she whispered to me.

"No," I said, laughing. "There was a certain smell that I remember from my dream. It's not here now."

"Maybe that's why they call them dreams, Bobby, because they're not real," Debbie harped.

I half-laughed at her joking, but my nightmare this time had been really scary. Debbie breathed in deeply. "The air's a lot better here than in Brooklyn, I'll tell you that," she said.

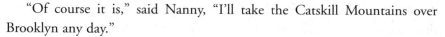

"Of course it is," said Nanny, "I'll take the Catskill Mountains over Brooklyn any day."

Beepa tucked me in bed and said, "Go to sleep now, Bobby. Ve'll go svimming tomorrow."

"I love to *svim*," Debbie mimicked.

"You go to bed," Beepa barked, chastising Deb for making fun of his accent. I knew I couldn't look at Debbie or I would burst out laughing. As soon as she was out the door, I heard her laugh out loud. Beepa looked at me with a stern look, then smiled and we laughed together. He brushed the hair back from my forehead and patted me on the head. "Tomorrow ve'll go svimming," he whispered, and winked at me as he turned out the light and closed the door behind him. Spending my summers in the mountains was memorable, but my roots were in Brooklyn, New York. I come from a diverse ethnic background.

My father is Italian, with a little Brazilian mixed in. My mother is Scandinavian, half Norwegian and half Swedish. I came into this world on November 28, 1960, at Madison Park Hospital in Brooklyn, New York, a good ol' American mix of all of the above—the original Swedish meat ball. I was the second of three children born to Attilio Nunzio and Greta Carlson Petrocelli. Dad was no dummy. He married a blonde Scandinavian beauty. That's my pops. Attilio "Duke." Duke is what his friends called him. He got the name as a boy because he was always fighting in the schoolyard. "Put up your dukes," he would tell the other boys. Almost everyone growing up in Brooklyn had a nickname. My dad's closest friends were Philly "Bumble" and Freddie "The Crow." Bumble got his name because he just looks like a "bumble," which is someone who is big, strong, hairy, and tough. Freddie got his when he came back to Brooklyn after the war with an army jacket with the name Crow sewn on it. You would've expected a more colorful story with a nickname like "The Crow." Me? I was called "Pet" or "Petro"—short for Petrocelli. Anybody else in Brooklyn saddled with a normal name got a "y" tacked to its end. You know, like Tony, or Joey, or Franky, or Suzy. Nicknames defined who you were. They all end in "Y."

My father was from a middle-class, blue-collar, Catholic background. He worked two jobs. His main job was with the New York City Transit

Authority as a subway track foreman and inspector. He also worked part-time as a security guard at Madison Square Garden. A typical day for him was to work from early morning until four o'clock in the afternoon, come home, gobble down some dinner, and go to the Garden or to the stadium. During the summer months he worked at both Yankee and Shea stadiums.

My father worked hard for our family which helped me realize the importance of earning an honest living. He got that from his family. His parents were immigrants from Italy. They got off the boat on Ellis Island, then traveled west, and finally settled in the blue-collar Pittsburgh area before Grandpa Attilio followed his brother to Brooklyn. Grandma Louise could cook some incredible Italian food. She was legendary for her authentic, mouth-watering pasta dishes. And her special way of cooking every type of fish in the sea was known far and wide. My dad would tell me what a stern man his father was, but he did whatever he could to provide for his large family of seven siblings. Dad told me that while he was growing up, he and his brothers would do whatever they could to help provide for the family. My dad spent years shining shoes to help the family get by in those tough times. He would give most of the money he made to his parents and was only able to keep ten cents for himself. "Bobby," he told me, "You can't brown-nose your way into anything. You have to work hard to achieve your goals. Don't ever be phony. Always be yourself. Don't try to be someone you're not. People can see right through it. But if you're honest and true to who you are, people will respect you for being a man, a real man." My mother would tell me, "Bobby, if you want to achieve things in life, you have to be willing to work hard. Then you can do anything you want to do."

My parents' hard work finally paid off—they achieved "The American Dream"—to move out of our apartment on 24th Avenue and 86th Street in Bensonhurst and move into our very own home, a house on East 24th Street in the nearby neighborhood of Sheepshead Bay. What some people might not know is that owning a house, actually owning and not renting in New York, is a huge, huge success. When you hear all the stories of New Yorkers and the incredibly high rents they have to pay, you know why: Most of them cannot buy anything because of the incredible expense, so they rent. It's not uncommon for families to rent an apartment or if they're lucky, one floor of a house for their entire lifetime. So this ownership of a house for my parents was a major accomplishment. Ask any New Yorker and they'll tell you. It's a big deal to own something there. It was an average two-story house in a middle-class neighborhood. My parents did like so many other homeowners do, even to this day; they rented out the first-floor apartment to another family. We had three bedrooms upstairs: my parents had one, my sisters, Debbie and Chrissy had one, and I had the smallest one—in the front of the house facing the street. The house didn't have air conditioning so I lay awake on summer nights, unable to sleep because of the heat. I recall always being in desperate search for the cool side of the pillow and I heard everything—I do mean everything that went on in the street—dogs barking, cats fighting, horns blowing, couples arguing, parents yelling, teenagers carrying on while they roamed the streets. I heard and saw it all. The best thing that I saw from my window, though, were the people in my neighborhood sitting out on the stoops in front of their houses. In Brooklyn, the "stoop was our world." People sat for hours on end enjoying their favorite beverage, watching the world unfold. The view from the stoop was our daily entertainment. For yutes ("youthsss" as some might pronounce it), the stoop was their playing field. Stoop ball, stick ball, box ball, red-light green-light, 1-2-3, and what-ever new game we devised.

My mom was from a middle-class, charismatic-Christian background. She worked an office job before my sisters and I were born. Once she started the family, however, she felt that it was important to stay home and raise the kids. But as we got older, she returned to work at Alexander's department store.

Both my parents worked hard to instill discipline, morals, and values in our lives. Certain things were just flat-out expected of us, and if we didn't obey, or if we answered back, we were in trouble. I mean big trouble. We were each responsible for certain chores, whether it was running to the store, taking out the garbage, shoveling snow, or cleaning up after dinner. We knew what was expected of us and each child did their share.

When dinner was at 5:30, it did not mean we could show up at 5:35. We had to be prompt—no straggling was allowed. Dinnertime was set and that was that. We all ate together as a family. As I look back, I'm glad we did. Those memories of sharing that time together on a regular basis are a part of my foundation today. I love to hear that families still eat dinner together. On the afternoons when I was at the park and lost track of time, out of nowhere I would hear my dad whistle the famous "Petrocelli whistle." It was like a special call that meant, "You better get your butt home for dinner right now, or you're not going to have a butt to bring home for dinner no more." I ran as fast as I could with my feet hitting my butt. When the whistle blew, my legs instinctively turned toward home and began running.

When we got to the kitchen, we all had assigned seats at the table: my father on my left, my mom across from me nearest to the stove, Debbie to my right, and Chrissy between my parents. Mom would serve up macaroni, meatballs, Italian sausage, and a salad. Before we ate, my father always said the same prayer. We knew it so well that we mouthed the words as he repeated it time and time again. He prayed, "Dear Jesus, bless the food we are about to receive and thank You, thank You, thank You, for blessing us and blessing our home. We thank You in Jesus' name. Amen." We especially loved when he got to the part, "and thank You, thank You, thank You… " There was a rhythm to it, like a cadence. When he came to that part, I would look at Debbie for the first thank You, my mother for the second, and Chrissy for the third. Sometimes I changed the order.

After dinner my father would send me to the local candy store, luncheonette, and five-and-dime to get our favorite candy. Our locals were called Abe and Harold's, and Ruby. "Bobby, run down to the store and get me Butterfingers, Clark bars and Mary Janes." These were Dad's favorites. The rest of us enjoyed M & Ms, Almond Joys, Nestle Crunch, Chunky, candy cigarettes, wax bottle sheets of candy with the little dots, Bazooka bubble gum, and of course the baseball cards with the stick of gum in every pack. You get the picture. That was our after-dinner treat. There wasn't a better way to wash down a good meal than with our favorite sweets. We loved them all. It's the little things like that that I remember so well. I can still see my father lean back from the table, reach his big hand into his right-hand pants pocket, and hear the sweet sound of change jingling around. Somehow the melodic sound of pocket change always brought instant anticipatory smiles to our faces. To a kid, pocket change equals candy. It's one of the greatest sounds for a child to hear. He didn't have to say a word—we were already smiling before he said what he wanted. It was a magical, simple pleasure—such a simple time. Time with your family goes so quickly, and once it's gone, you can never get it back. The years move on without our permission.

Becky, an old Jewish woman in her late sixties, used to baby-sit us. She lived next door to us, so it wasn't a problem for her to come over and watch us once in a while when my parents wanted to have an evening out. Becky was sweet, but sometimes she had that musty, trunk-in-the-attic smell about her. Debbie would coax me to look up her dress or to make fun of her runny nose, and then when my parents came home she would be right by the door. "Bobby was making fun of Becky tonight. He was looking up her dress and laughing at her," she'd say.

When it came to being punished, my sisters and I did not get a choice like other kids in the neighborhood did. We were both spanked *and* grounded—a double whammy. It would have been nice to have one or the other, but not with *my* parents. I even remember begging them, "Please, just spank me, but don't make me stay in my room all day." I would rather have taken a little more spanking than get double punishment. But when it came to discipline, my parents did not play around. My father always made it clear to my sisters and me that he didn't want to ever hear that we had done anything to disgrace the Petrocelli name. We were never to embarrass the family. Discipline was important to my parents because it taught us respect. It also taught us that we were expected to do what was right, and if we made the wrong choice, there would be consequences to pay. We were responsible for our actions. This was one of the most important things my parents ever taught us—responsibility.

My sister Debbie is three and a half years my elder. Chrissy is seven years younger than me. Because of the gap in age difference between Chrissy and me, we never had much in common growing up. When Chrissy was in first grade, I was in eighth and Debbie was in the eleventh grade. That was a huge difference at that time in our lives. As an adult, seven and ten years doesn't seem so much, but to a child time is different. Debbie and I found trouble together when we picked on Chrissy. I remember, one time we even tied her up with telephone wire and left her in the closet, then when my mother got home... Even so, I was still Chrissy's older brother. I took her to the park and out for ice cream. At the park, I'd tell the other kids, "This is my sister. You mess with her, you mess with me." When you're thirteen and your sister is six, it's easy to feel protective. I was a senior in high school when Chrissy was in fifth grade. As we've gotten older and become adults, we have grown much closer, and are now very active in each other's lives.

Both Christmas and Thanksgiving hold special memories. Our Thanksgiving table was always full. Besides the usual turkey and dressing, Nanny also cooked her special Norwegian dishes, which were incredible. We couldn't fit one more chair around that old wooden table of Nanny's. The meal was loud, full of energy, and exciting. I can still smell Nanny's home-made stuffing and almond green beans, the turkey with giblet gravy, and I can taste the brown sugar on the sweet potatoes. I could never get enough of her cooking, but I often tried. Thanksgiving was more than a meal together—it was a celebration, an event, a gathering of the relatives to be thankful for the lives we had been given and our many blessings. It was a joyous time when we felt a real freedom to laugh and enjoy each other's company. I can't imagine Thanksgiving any other way.

Most of my summers were spent at Nanny and Beepa's summer home in Lexington, New York, in the Catskill Mountains with my Uncle Artie and cousins Roy, Billy, and Allen. It was an experience my Brooklyn friends could only imagine. We swam in refreshing, sparkling streams, jumping off ropes and bridges into the cool water below. We camped, fished, hiked, and explored ghost towns in the mountains. At least once a week we went to the drive-in movies. "It's my turn to sit in the back seat. You got to last time," I would tell my cousins, even though sometimes I had sat back there the time before. To sit out in the open air and watch a movie under the stars is something I'll never forget. There was something really cool about the little speaker that you'd hang in your window. The sound was absolutely terrible, but the fact that you had to hang the speaker on the car made it special— you knew you were at a drive-in movie! "There's a little man in that speaker," my father told us. "Where do you think the voice is coming from?" The fact was, we didn't know, but we kept looking for him.

Getting fresh milk at the dairy farm was something we couldn't do in Brooklyn. Debbie and I would laugh and laugh at the smell of the barn.

Somehow, the smell of manure gave us the giggles, and once we started laughing, we couldn't stop.

"Bobby, was that you? You stink," Debbie would say, holding her nose. "There's your twin right there," she would add as she pointed to the ugliest cow on the farm, slobbering and chewing on its cud.

"If that's my twin, then that's also your brother," I would snap back. Then she would chase me down and stuff hay down my back. If I was lucky, I would get her first—but she always made me pay later.

People don't believe me when I tell them I grew up on grits. Nanny cooked them almost every morning. And before we went to sleep at night, she would wash our feet. It must have been a custom she had brought with her from Norway. "Nanny, I'm ready," I would tell her each night, and then she would wash my feet, dry them, and tuck me into bed.

Many summers we piled into Uncle Artie's station wagon and drove across the country to visit my mother's brother in Washington State. Five different summers we traveled from New York to Loomis, Washington, to visit my mother's brother David and my cousins David, Danny, and Tania. Along the way we visited the Rocky Mountains, Mount Rushmore, San Francisco, Yosemite National Park, American Indian reservations, and the Smokey Mountains. I got to see a lot of country that many of my friends, most of whom spent their summers in Brooklyn, had never seen. When I would return to Brooklyn and tell my friends of my adventures in the western wilderness, they would never believe me. Plus the fact that I grew up eating grits was beyond belief. The experience of traveling so much as a child gave me an appreciation for our beautiful country and the rich history, customs, and traditions of the different parts of the United States. I believe the "bug" I have for traveling and adventure was birthed during those years. Family is important.

The Petrocellis have always stressed the importance of family (A La Familia). Two of my father's brothers, David and Vincent, lived near us in Sheepshead Bay, so I got to spend a lot of time with my cousins Mary Jo, Vinny and Tony. (You should know by now that all true Italian families have a cousin Vinny, and Tony). The reason why all Italian families have several Tony's in them is because when all our relatives were coming from Italy to New York, the only way they knew where they were going was from the fact that they literally had the word *TONY* stamped on their forehead. *TONY* meant "TO NY" (New York). Mary Jo, Vinny, and I were the same age so we were in school together. Spending time at Uncle Davey's and Uncle Vinny's houses meant eating great Italian cooking. Aunt Dottie and Aunt Lucille cooked some unbelievable Italian dishes: chicken cutlet parmigiana, manicotti, pasta specialties, you name it, they make my mouth water just thinking about it. They always made you feel special and loved. In Italian families there is always so much food to eat. You know the old jokes about the Italian Momma saying, "Mange, Mange, Mange!" It's true. In Italian families you are not allowed to leave the table until you eat so much that you have to open up your belt. Italians don't eat until they're full; we eat until we're tired then we take a nap. An hour later the smell of food wakes us up and we're ready to start all over again. Even now, during the holidays when I return to New York, I look forward to seeing family and enjoying their wonderful delicacies. My dad's oldest brother, Tony, and sister Flo lived outside of Brooklyn. It is still so wonderful when all the families get together for the holidays or special occasions.

The youngest of the Petrocelli brothers is my Uncle Rico who lived outside Boston with my Aunt Elsie and their four sons. Uncle Rico, a professional baseball player, was a Boston Red Sox All-Star. He truly made the family proud. In 1961, after graduating from Sheepshead Bay High School in Brooklyn, he signed as a free agent. From 1965 to 1977 he played shortstop and third base for the Boston Red Sox. He helped lead the Red Sox to two World Series appearances—in 1967 against the St. Louis Cardinals and in 1975 against the Cincinnati Reds. Until the Red Sox finally reversed the curse of Babe Ruth in 2004, the Series of 1975 was still considered the greatest World Series of all time as future Hall of Famer Carlton Fisk hit that dramatic home run in the bottom of the twelfth inning of game six to win the game and send it to an awesome game seven. Against the Cardinals Uncle Rico hit two home runs in one game. In the '75 series, he batted over .300 to help the Red Sox get to a seventh game. Four times he was named an American League All-Star, and in 1969 he hit forty home runs, which was eventually broken thirty years later by the former Seattle Mariner shortstop Alex Rodriquez.

Watching Uncle Rico play while I was growing up was really exciting. You would always catch me following him on television or the radio or in box scores in the newspaper. Uncle Rico will never know what kind of effect he had on my friends. When he did well, they were quiet and subdued. But when he had a bad game or wasn't playing well, they gave me a hard time. "Hey, Bobby—your Uncle Rico struck out last night with the bases loaded. What happened to him? Even I could've hit the ball somewhere," one would say.

"Oh, yeah," I'd say. "At least my uncle is a baseball player—not like yours, who works in the sewers." They would forget the great things he would do.

The greatest thrill of all was going to Yankee Stadium and Boston's Fenway Park to watch him play. I remember sitting in the dugout and locker room before the games, looking out onto the field, and thinking about great players from the past. I even had the privilege of meeting legends like Mickey Mantle, Joe Pepitone, Whitey Ford, Carl Yazstremski, Jim Lonborg, and Carlton Fisk.

One particular Saturday in 1967 when I was six, I went to Yankee Stadium to watch my Uncle Rico play in an early afternoon game. It had been cloudy all morning. When I walked into the stadium—and I'll never forget this—the minute I stepped onto the field, a beam of light lit up the right field bleachers. I looked up in the sky and the sun looked like a huge spotlight. It was as if someone had hit a switch and made the sun shine through, right on cue. The smell of the freshly cut green grass in the outfield was invigorating. I looked out at the magnificence of the place and stood motionless and awestruck.

My father's voice brought me back to earth when he said, "Bobby, come here for a minute." I walked backwards toward the dugout, still trying to take in the magnitude of Yankee Stadium and the echoes of greatness that I heard throughout the place. I felt myself getting near the dugout and when I turned, my dad said, "Bobby, I'd like you to meet Carl Yazstremski." Before I knew it, I was face to face and shaking hands with Carl Yazstremski. *The* Carl Yazstremski. *Yaz.* Then, in an instant, my dad was walking with Uncle Rico and escorting me to the Yankee dugout. Sitting right in front of me was Mickey Mantle. *The Mick.* He said, "Hi," and shook my hand as if I were a real person. Next I met Whitey Ford, the Yankees' pitching ace. I remember saying to myself, I hope someday I can play here and be just like Uncle Rico. He actually knew these guys on a first-name basis. I thought to myself, I don't care what my friends say about my Uncle Rico. Their uncles don't personally know Mickey Mantle or Carl Yazstremski or Joe Pepitone or Whitey Ford. They can laugh all they want. I hoped they had seen me on TV. As I grew in age I would always meet my favorites of the day: Luis Tiant, Carlton Fisk, and Fred Lynn.

I was about seven when I got interested in athletics, especially baseball. With an uncle as a pro ball player and a father working at professional sports facilities, I developed a great love for the game. Not only did I watch Uncle Rico play, but Dad took me to stadiums when he worked. I saw the Yankees and Mets play all the time, with greats like Tom Seaver, Willie Mays, Hank Aaron, and two of my all-time favorites, Nolan Ryan and Reggie Jackson. I watched the Knicks and Rangers play at Madison Square Garden.

From that time on I enjoyed competitive athletics. Most of my athletic talent was developed at a park one block from my house where my friends and I played touch football, hardball on the concrete (I actually used hard-balls signed by Hall of Famers like Mickey Mantle and destroyed the balls!), basketball, and every form of stickball you can imagine.

If we didn't go to the park, we played on the stoop or right in the middle of the street. We used manhole covers as the goal lines for football. The side-walks were the out-of-bounds area. The telephone wires were our goal posts. Garbage pails (steel trash cans) were used for basketball hoops. Somebody's mother was always complaining about missing a broom handle, or two… or three… or four.

We even played hardball in the middle of the street. We really didn't break too many windshields. Denting cars, now that was another story. "You kids go and play in front of your own house," Mrs. Wolfe, a neighbor, would yell down at us. Then she would hose down the street in front of her house so that it was too slick for us to play there.

And we played hockey. We put on steel skates, the ones that fit over sneakers and had a key so you could tighten them.

During baseball season, I often got into arguments with my close friend Bruno. Bruno's full name was Oreste Frank Bruno, but "Bruno" was his nickname. When you think of someone named Bruno, you probably think of a big, burly guy, six-foot-four and 250 pounds of muscle. Bruno didn't come close to fitting that description. He was short and skinny. We did everything together—played ball, went to school, joked around, hung out, threw snowballs at people from the top of his apartment building, you name it. One thing we did a lot was argue about which team was better, the Yankees or the Red Sox. Now you have to understand, Bruno was a big-time Yankee fan. I was a Red Sox fan. Our arguments got so heated that I'm surprised we remained best friends.

While playing ball, my friends and I emulated our favorite athletes. I would add my nickname to their already famous name. During football season I would be called "Joe Willie Pet" (Namath) and "O.J. Pet" (Simpson). Out in the street playing football, I would drop back to pass a long bomb to Bruno, announcing my own play-by-play: "Joe Willie Pet back to pass. He's being chased by Merlin Olsen. He scrambles—breaks one tackle. Butkus is in hot pursuit. Joe Willie Pet sees Bruno in the end zone by Mrs. Wolfe's house. The street is dry and clear. Here's the pass—a perfect spiral towards Bruno all alone. *He caught it! Touchdown! What a great athletic effort from Joe Willie Petro. Harrrrrrrrr! Way to go, Listen to that crowd, ladies and gentlemen."*

Eventually baseball became my number-one sport. I began dreaming of following in my uncle's footsteps. He had been a neighborhood hero. Everybody knew who he was—a local boy who "done good." I was starting to develop myself. Slowly, but surely, I began to hear the whispers. "That young Petrocelli boy ain't a bad ballplayer." Since I played at the same high school that Uncle Rico had, I was quickly gaining the reputation of being "Rico Petrocelli's nephew," but was making a name for myself as an outfielder. There wasn't a fly ball I didn't think I could chase down. Playing with future major leaguers like John Franco, I began to think about the possibility of someday playing pro ball.

Faith (I don't like to use the word religion) played a major role in my formative years. My parents felt it was essential that attending church regularly from an early age and understanding the importance of God was essential.

Pastor Emanuel Greco, before he died, was a true role model. Not only was he the pastor of our church, but he had a family and was a New York City school teacher. He always showed me respect and love.

"Bobby, how're things going for you?" he would ask.

"Not too bad, Pastor."

"'Not too bad' can mean a lot of things, Bobby," he said, "'Not too bad' can mean 'they could be better,' or it can mean 'they could be worse.' Which one is it?"

He wanted you to be real and to cut through the bull. He was always interested in seeing what was really happening and would not just accept superficial responses. He was genuinely interested in people. Very rarely do you find a pastor with such genuine concern for his flock. That's why he was influential in my life, more than he would ever know. During my junior year at college, Pastor Greco even sent me seven hundred dollars of his own money to help me with tuition. His actions spoke as loudly as his words. He was a man of true integrity and genuine love for others.

Some of my closest friends were at our church: Joey Greco, Vinny DeLuzio, and Jay Ferraro. Yes, we called each other by our regular names—not Joey "The Steeple" Greco, or Vinny "The Sanctuary" DeLuzio, or Jay "The Pulpit" Ferraro. We could be just who we were in church. Though we were from different parts of Brooklyn, we were all active together in our church group. It was kind of cool for me to talk to them and find out what was happening in other parts of the "Big Apple." We spent a lot of time together. We knew that we wanted God to be an integral part of our lives.

The four of us also spent time together outside of church. We rode bikes along the Belt Parkway up to the Verrazzano Bridge, bowled together, went into Manhattan, or just hung out laughing hysterically. I especially liked when the whole church group went out to eat. I guess after learning about faith you get hungry. Have you ever noticed that in many different faiths, after going to temple or parish or church, everyone's ready to eat? And in New York we had places to eat. Boy, did we have places to eat! Any kind of food you wanted from every ethnic background—Italian, Jewish, Chinese, German, Polish, whatever. It was so convenient—you could sit in the restaurant or get it to go. Potato knishes, calzones, White Castle hamburgers, submarine heroes, pizza—food from every ethnic background, and of all these great foods, we had the choice of the greatest pizza in the world, center cuts of Sicilian pizza from the famed Spumoni Gardens in Brooklyn. There's nothing like washing it down with a large cup of spumoni. So many pizzerias—there weren't enough days in the week to enjoy all of it.

My mother and father loved good food. They always emphasized that anything worthwhile takes a lot of work. Whether cooking your favorite dish or fulfilling your dreams. It takes effort. Things were not just handed to us. We had to earn it or save for it. When I was old enough, not only did I make a buck for myself, but I also gained a true sense of responsibility and pride that comes with it. During my younger days, I looked forward to a snowstorm, going from door to door and making a couple of bucks for shoveling people's walks or driveways. In high school, the most memorable part-time job that I ever had was at Ruby's Luncheonette. It was a corner food establishment with a lunch counter and stools. Ruby's served sandwiches, soups, salads, and fountain drinks. They also served the most famous drink of all— the Egg Cream. Ruby's was known all over Brooklyn for making the best egg creams. (No, there aren't eggs in them.) There's a secret to a great egg cream. It takes milk, but the milk must be icy. Add chocolate syrup with a touch of vanilla syrup, stir in the seltzer water—and *viola.*

I worked as the clean-up crew, washing pots, pans, stoves, ovens, cleaning grills and windows. It was a rewarding feeling to work hard and bring home my minimum wage of $2.10 an hour. There's something gratifying about doing an honest day's work. The work ethic established at Ruby's has always left me with the feeling of accomplishment and a job well done. There was a sense of pride attached to working for an establishment like Ruby's. Because he took pride in his work and his food, I could take pride in my work. I respected Ruby for working hard to make his place the best it could be and for the reputation he had as one of the best luncheonettes in all of Brooklyn. I was proud to tell people that I worked at Ruby's.

My parents encouraged us to be independent and to experience as much of life as we could. My youth was filled with a number of diverse, positive experiences. My mother stressed the importance of working hard in everything that I did. She told me, "You can do anything that you want to do, be who you want to be, achieve your dreams and goals. But remember, anything in life that is worthwhile will take hard work and dedication." I knew I had to be willing to give my best if I were to fulfill my dreams. Those words echo in my heart now more than ever.

My parents tried to give me the best of everything, stressing to me the importance of family and faith, the need for integrity and honesty, and to always do the right thing—always—and to show respect and kindness to everyone, especially to adults.

The opportunity of growing up in the city and spending valuable time in the country gave me a well-rounded perspective for living life to the fullest. My parents instilled in me a sense of morals, values, and integrity that truly helped build a strong foundation in my life. With this foundation intact, I could face anything that would come my way.

CHAPTER

College Days

Following outstanding baseball seasons at Sheepshead Bay High School, I opted to enroll in Oral Roberts University, a small NCAA Division I school in Tulsa, Oklahoma. I had liked ORU from an early age. Every Sunday morning I'd watch Oral Roberts' program on television while we got ready for church. I was drawn to the school by his compassion and genuine concern for others. I'd look at his beautiful college campus on television and say, "That's where I want to go someday." I particularly liked their emphasis on physical fitness along with academics and spiritual growth. Besides that, the campus was spectacular on television. It looked like an exciting place to be. My mother supported and encouraged me in my choice.

Many of my peers coming out of high school played at St. John's University and other powerhouse baseball programs on the East Coast. A few signed right away with pro teams and reported to their farm clubs, hoping to work their way up to the major leagues within a few years. I loved baseball, but I already knew that I wanted something more, something that baseball couldn't give—something deep inside my heart.

Oral Roberts University is not for everybody. Plain and simple, it is a Christian institution with strict rules, excellence in academics, athletics, and spirituality. And unless you were there only to please your parents, you were willing to accept that certain behaviors were not tolerated. Those behaviors were defined by the Honor Code, which was spelled out clearly at the beginning of each school year.

The Honor Code was a document we were all required to sign. It listed a set of specific things that we would agree to do, or not to do. I can't remember anyone leaving for refusing to sign, yet many students signed knowing that they would at one point or another break it. The Honor Code established a sense of responsible conduct for the students. We were discouraged from drinking alcohol, using drugs, having premarital sex, cheating, plagiarizing copy, falsifying, or being dishonest or deceitful in any way. None of us were perfect but tried our best to abide by these guidelines.

The dress code called for men to wear a shirt and tie to class, to Chapel, and to the cafeteria during specified hours during the week. Women had to wear skirts or dresses during the same periods. But it wasn't as bad as it seems. The general level of cleanliness and personal hygiene at ORU was high. On the weekends, we dressed casually around campus and could roll out of bed and into the cafeteria with a mattress head and sweats on. But most of the time we tried to look presentable. I respected that. I've had friends in other schools that didn't have a dress code and it was a completely different ball game. Some people today don't care what they look like, but with such an emphasis on appearance and image these days, more young people could use this kind of dress code.

I arrived on campus in the fall of 1978 with my mother, father, and

Chrissy in our 1973 blue Chevy Impala. The temperature was 107 in the shade, and the Impala didn't have air conditioning. When my parents and sister left me at school and started back to New York, I chased after the car, crying, as I ran down the Avenue of Flags that led into the university. It took some adjusting to get used to a small, relatively quiet town like Tulsa after being from the "city that never sleeps."

Tulsa was hot in August. When you stepped outside, the heat and humidity jumped on you. Stand outside for a few minutes and in no time you'd drop twenty-five to thirty pounds. I walked outside and the air was so hot that deep breaths burned my throat and lungs. I quickly learned to take shallow breaths.

After twelve hundred miles, I was here—in college. How could I not be excited? The campus was straight out of *Star Wars*. It was futuristic, shiny, and new. The buildings were nothing short of spectacular. The mood on campus was electric. It pulsated with an energy I can't explain. I guess it happens on every college campus at the beginning of each semester. There was an antici-pation—an air of expectation. As I walked across campus the first time, I saw new faces, fresh faces, smiling faces. I wasn't used to people being so friendly and smiley—big ole smiles with white teeth—not yellow, cigarette-stained, gap-toothed, nasty-teeth smiles like in Times Square. These people loved to smile. It was infectious, and the whole student body caught it.

But the biggest thing that struck me about the mood at ORU was a sincere, genuine feeling. People were happy to be there. People actually looked me in the eye. I wasn't used to that. Everybody said "Hello." One time while walking from one building to another I counted twenty-seven "hellos," eighteen "how's it goings," eleven "what's ups," five "howdys," three "nice to see ya's," and two "praise the Lords." They didn't have to yell at you to talk to you. You could have a civilized, person-to-person, no-holds-barred, quiet conversation. No horns blew, no taxis honked, Mrs. Corona wasn't yelling out the window for Mario and Nunzio to "come home for Spaghettios." You weren't worried about passing through another neighborhood and having somebody want to fight because you looked at them the wrong way.

The philosophy at ORU was simple: Help to make whole, healthy, complete, well-rounded people—healthy in body, mind, and spirit. Years later, it's finally coming out that this so-called "new" philosophy of being healthy in every aspect of life is vital to the health of our fast-paced society.

Being an athlete, I appreciated the emphasis on physical fitness. As it was the late '70s, the aerobics program at ORU was well ahead of its time. The fitness craze hadn't yet caught on. The idea at Oral Roberts University was to encourage athletics and other related physical activities to the point that they would become not only a necessity, but also a natural part of the students' lifestyles. I particularly liked the fact that so many of the women were serious about keeping in shape by running, doing aerobics, even swimming. Every guy knew that the girls looked great. Popular magazines, including *Playboy*, often rated our women among the best looking. We men at ORU quietly gloated about the accolades, even though it was officially against school policy to actually read *Playboy*. Since ORU was a religious institution, we had an honor code, or rather a set of moral standards to which we agreed to abide by while students. One of the rules was that we were forbidden to order and receive publications of this nature.

During my junior year someone wrote my name on a *Playboy* order card. When that first issue came to my box—the *only* issue to ever come to my mail slot—the mail lady was not amused.

"Young man, I don't know who you think you are, or what kind of background you come from, but we at Oral Roberts University do not and will not tolerate behavior like this. If you choose to continue to subscribe to this magazine, I will have you reported to the Dean of Men and recommend that he expel you from this school. Is that clear?" she asked.

"But, ma'am, I didn't subscribe to this magazine. Someone played a joke so I'd get in trouble," I pleaded.

"Do you boys think I'm stupid?" she said with her eyes narrowing and burning a hole straight through me.

"No, ma'am," I said.

"Fine. Then straighten up and fly right," she said as she closed the mailroom window, telling me that the conversation was now abruptly over.

Word spread quickly. Not word that I'd be expelled—who cares about that? But word that *Playboy* had actually come. The guys on my wing had a field day. "Petro, I heard you got some *good* mail today," one guy said with a big smile on his face. Another said, "Petro, I need some pictures for my anatomy presentation tomorrow! You got any I could borrow?" A third said, "Bobby, the dean called and wanted to know how our women rated this year. He's stopping by later to talk to you and also wants you to make an announcement in Chapel on Friday, okay?"

Can you imagine the university president standing up on the platform during the chapel service at a major Christian college—after twenty minutes of hymns, a scripture passage, and a seven-minute prayer—and saying, "I want to congratulate our female students' bodies—or rather the female student's body... Ahem, let me start again. I would like to congratulate our female student body for being rated No. 3 in *Playboy* magazine for having the third most beautiful women among universities in the U.S. We were only a few votes behind UCLA and Brigham Young, but we'll try harder next year, because, after all, isn't that what we're all about, being No. 1 in *Playboy* magazine?"

"*Haarrrrrrrrrr!*" responds the crowd, as the auditorium is whipped into a frenzy. After ten minutes, the celebration dies down just enough for the president to say, "Let's have the benediction, and don't forget to pick up your commemorative issue from Bobby Petrocelli at the door as you leave." There is thunderous applause. "Okay, please everybody. Bow your heads and pray with me. Our precious Heavenly... "

I thought that I was going to be kicked out of school for something I didn't do. They were brutal on me. I had been set up—big time. It wasn't that funny then, but I can laugh about it now. And I know exactly who sent it to me too—my friend Cheeks. He had a twisted sense of humor like that. I knew it was him.

Going away to school was one of the best things I ever did. I was away from my parents, away from my neighborhood, away from the safety and "comfort zone" I had known in my familiar surroundings. It forced me to become independent. This is how I grew. This is how I learned. This is how I matured.

Sometimes I felt as if I were the only freshman on the whole campus. I often strode confidently through the campus completely lost because I wanted to look as if I knew where I was going. Soon, though, the Law of Magnetic Ignorance kicked in. That's the unexplainable phenomenon that happens when two lost freshmen attract each other, then a third, and a fourth, and soon there's a pack, and then a mob, growing, feeding, searching, stuck together by class rank and ignorance. They roam together likes wolves, desperate to be accepted into the pack—the pack of ignorant freshmen.

Registration Day, August 1978, was not a planned experience.

"Where's the CC?" I sheepishly asked a guy, looking for the Classroom Center.

"You a freshman?" he said back at me with a little bit of an attitude.

I hesitated. "Yeah…" I felt like saying, "Yo, you got a problem with that?" but I didn't. The truth was, I *was* a freshman. I found out later that he was, too. He just said it in such a demeaning tone that I wouldn't have ever known.

Following his directions, I walked past the cafeteria and approached a white-domed building. As I got closer, I heard the noise inside getting stronger and louder. "Somebody's having a party here," I thought. I opened the door and stepped inside. It was nothing short of walking into the pit of the New York Stock Exchange. Registration. It was wild. Students frantically ran from one line to the next. I had absolutely no idea where to start. I surveyed the area and felt dizzy for a moment.

Finally, the Law of Magnetic Ignorance caught me and swept me to one side of the room where a sign read, "Start here." God must've had pity on me because I ended up in the right line. "Last name?" the woman behind the desk asked me.

"Petrocelli," I said.

She searched through the "P" section and pulled out a card with my name on it. "Robert J. Petrocelli?" she asked in a serious tone.

"Yes, ma'am," I replied in a little stronger voice this time.

"From Brooklyn, New York?" she asked.

"Yes, ma'am," I acknowledged.

She smiled as she handed me the card. It was a peculiar kind of smile, as if she knew something that I didn't—like she was saying, "You should be used to this craziness. You should feel right at home in this atmosphere." You know something? As stupid as this may seem, I did. It was the first thing to happen that reminded me of home. At that instant I grew about a foot taller, or rather my confidence did.

Freshmen registered last. By the time it was our turn after the seniors, juniors, and sophomores, we had to settle for whatever we could get. It was a rat race. Students ran from line to line trying to secure certain classes before they filled up. No one liked to get up on Monday morning and no one liked to be stuck in class on Friday afternoons. I registered for the 7:50 a.m. classes since these were the classes nobody wanted. I didn't mind, though. I like getting up early and don't mind early morning classes. I never could lie in bed all day. I'm an early bird. It's in my nature to be driven and to get things done. I didn't find many other students who thought quite the same way.

Studies didn't come easy at ORU, but I learned *how* to study. My freshman year was my weakest, and I managed to reach just below a "B" average. I improved my sophomore year and pulled my grades up every year after that. ORU was not the type of school that you could do nothing and expect to pass classes. Even the general education classes that everyone had to take were tough. There were no freebies. None. Zip. *Notta.*

ORU definitely wasn't a party school. Professors took attendance in every class and cutting class dropped your grade. A lot of students complained about the attendance policy, but I'm glad ORU had it. It showed the administration cared that we got the best education possible. Some of my friends at state schools laughed when I told them about the attendance policy, but they weren't in school to learn. They were there to have a good time. "That's what college is for," they said. "Party time." Hey, I had a great time in college. It all depends on the people with whom you associate. You choose your own friends. You have to make sure you choose them well. You can party without abusing substances.

The friends I made at ORU are still some of my best friends today. We lived together, laughed together, pretended to study together, ate together, played together, prayed together, worked together, struggled financially together... You get the picture.

I knew from the start of my sophomore year that I wanted to be a teacher and coach, so I declared health and physical education as my major. I had never had a coach whom I really looked up to or admired, and I wanted to be the coach I had never had. I loved the physical education classes, but the toughest ones were the health and science courses. They were *work*. Anatomy and physiology were monsters. Pre-med majors and nursing students definitely had my sympathy. If that's what they wanted to do, God bless them. I'd gladly coach their children.

I was fortunate to live with guys who had it all: athleticism, good looks, brains, and a love of God. Most of all, they knew how to have a good time. We had a lot of good times. Not the kind that you think you enjoy while you're doing it—like getting drunk out of your mind and then not being able to remember what you did. I'm talking about memorable, funny, off-the-wall things that I still laugh about now, years later. The memories are still vivid in my mind, as if they had happened just yesterday—memories and friendships that I wouldn't trade for anything in the world.

Jay Ferraro was one of those friends. I called him "House" because he was a massive guy, a huge bodybuilder. I knew Jay through church back in Brooklyn, and he came to ORU because of my description of the school. We roomed together my junior and senior years. Jay was studious and disciplined, probably from his weight-training work ethic. Craig Olson was another buddy I met when I first started school. He was from Nebraska and got me to fall in love with the Cornhuskers. He was a good athlete, had a great sense of humor, and was a good student—although he spent a lot of time at the registrar's office declaring a new major. Craig was in charge of hiring personnel for special retreats called Seminars that the university hosted, and managed to get me a lot of campus jobs.

Dave "Riv" Rivera was my resident advisor. Riv was from the Spanish Harlem section of New York and had attended the prestigious New York City Performing Arts high school of music and art on which they based the movie and television show "Fame." Riv was an exceptional athlete and basketball player. He carried himself as a Latin lover-type and had a lot of girls after him. He was very, very cool and used to drive the girls crazy with his slow, romantic eyes. John "Jakey" Jones is the only guy I know who gave himself his own nickname. He came into school as a freshman with Jay and Cheeks in 1980, my junior year. Jakey was from North Carolina and, to this day, won't admit that he wore cowboy boots and a leather belt with his name on it. Actually I now have in my possession that very belt buckle to prove it. Jakey was deceptively smart despite his southern accent that Riv couldn't understand. He too was a former high school star athlete, a great football player and running back until he tore up his knee. He had a way of charming the girls and we joked with him about "lipping up" on too many. Joe Liberatore came out of high school as one of the most heralded baseball players in the entire state of Indiana. He and Don Mattingly of the New York Yankees were among the top players in the state. Joe was recruited by ORU and played outfield for the Titans. I still joke with him about hitting a Roger Clemens fastball off of the centerfield fence in a game against the University of Texas. Joe and I became close while we were teammates on the baseball team.

Cheeks was another good friend at ORU. Half Filipino, full jokester, he was born in New York City but grew up in inner-city Pittsburgh. His real name was Chris, but got the name "Cheeks" from antics he pulled his freshman year so I'll let you figure out why his name is Cheeks. He was always laughing and joking and messing around at other people's expense. He was either just messing around, or playing basketball and messing around. He, along with my other buddies, were the type of guys who would do anything for you. They would give you the shirt off their back. Most people are lucky to have one friend like that. I had many of them. It's cool to look back at all the wonderful friends and acquaintances I made at ORU—too many to name and even remember.

When I think about them now, I realize we did some crazy things in school—nothing really to hurt anyone, but a lot of off-the-wall, funny, mischievous things. If it happened to be your birthday, we might jump you in the room, strip you naked, tie your hands and feet, put you in a fold-up rollaway bed, and close the bed with your feet hanging out one end and your chest and head hanging out the other. Then we'd wheel you over in front of one of the women's dorms and park you there with a big red ribbon tied around the bed and sing a rousing rendition of "Happy Birthday" to you. You were on your own to get back to the dorm unless you could convince an innocent female bystander to help you. But we strongly discouraged any good Samaritans for at least ten or fifteen minutes. After that, we were as helpful as can be—especially with summoning help. We would shout, "Come on, girls. Who wants to help the birthday boy?" By that time you wished that it wasn't your birthday anymore. And you were wishing you had more clothes on than just your birthday suit.

We also had wing wars when one wing of the dorm declared war on another. These were anything from shaving-cream battles to water fights. During one massive water fight with a wing downstairs, our wing drenched their entire floor and soaked most of their rooms. When the downstairs wing tried to retaliate, they made a tactical error by coming up the elevator. As soon as the elevator door opened, everyone inside was deluged with a typhoon of water. Wave after wave, we hit them until an inch of water stood on the floor. The poor guys kept hitting the button for the door to close, but what they didn't know was that we had put a piece of duct tape over the button on the hallway elevator button, so there was absolutely no way to close the door. When they finally realized what we had done, it was much too late. Poor guys, I heard they didn't dry out for a week. They never attacked us again.

During winters, ice and sleeting rainstorms are usual for Oklahoma, but accumulating snow is more rare. When it did come down, classes were canceled, and we went sledding on cafeteria trays and had brutal snowball fights. These snowball fights were greatly discouraged because someone was always getting hurt or hit in the eye, but we loved them. The best one we ever had was in January 1982. It had snowed all afternoon and the snow was perfect for snowballs. The temperature wasn't too cold, around twenty-nine or thirty degrees, and it was a wet snow. The snowballs packed easily and they packed well. It started off rather innocently in front of the cafeteria where a few guys from Towers dorms started throwing at guys from EMR, my dorm. As more and more guys came out of the cafeteria and joined in, however, the action started to heat up. Guys weren't just out to hit someone, they were out to "tattoo" one another, all in the name of pride for the dorm in which they lived. I compare it with the pride you feel in being from a certain neighborhood or city.

I was with Jay, Jakey, and Cheeks when we came out of the cafeteria and saw what was happening. Jay said, "Look, it's a snowball fight!" By the time he got to the word "snowball," Jakey and Cheeks were already down the steps, across the sidewalk and had three snowballs each in their hands. Jay and I quickly followed and ran across the same sidewalk and into the parking lot where the battle was starting to take shape.

Jakey and Cheeks were crazy. That's all you need to know about them. They just wanted to hit somebody. I saw them hit about five guys with snowballs before they realized their targets were from our own dorm. By this time, the snowball fight had grown to about ten against ten with more joining in. The parking lot was a perfect battlefield. There was plenty of fresh snow on the ground and on the cars, and you could use the vehicles as shields while reloading ammunition.

"Petro, look out!" Cheeks yelled as I got hit in the leg with an iceball.

"Owww," I said. It stung, and that's what got me into the battle. Jay, Jakey, Cheeks, and I alternated making and flipping snowballs to each other to maximize our firepower. The EMR guys made a forward surge and began pushing the Towers boys across the parking lot toward the Towers dorm. By now both forces had grown to about fifty men each. We kept firing and ducking, firing and ducking, firing and ducking—preparing to advance in a massive wave of furiously thrown snowballs.

"You ready to go, Jay?" I yelled.

"Let's do it, Bobby," Jay immediately snapped back at me.

I peered over the snow-covered Jeep that I had been ducking behind and saw a continuous barrage of white iceball-like missiles flying through the air in every direction.

"Pet, we hit seven guys each already, and you're still making your ammo," Jakey jabbed at me.

"Yeah, but five of those guys were from *our* dorm," I yelled back.

Jakey just smiled a toothy smile to let me know he didn't care who he hit, just as long as he hit somebody. Cheeks stood up and fired four snowballs in a row. Three hit one guy in the back. "That's what I'm talking about, right there! Three-for-four."

Cheeks and Jakey were getting into this a little too much, acting like Marines spearheading frontal assaults. A snowball whizzed by my head.

"Let's *go!*" Cheeks yelled as he led another surge. Jay and I grabbed four snowballs each and sprinted about twenty-five yards to the front line where Jakey and Cheeks were firing away like madmen. Thirty guys followed as we started to drive the Towers boys up the hill toward their dorm. When the rest of our guys saw the wall pushing them back, they all joined in. We bombarded them continuously and mercilessly. We had them pinned in and they had absolutely nowhere to run and no way to escape. It was like a firing squad as guys got hit with two and three snowballs at a time.

All at once we heard whistles blow down in the parking lot behind us. Five campus security guards ran confidently across the parking lot in formation blowing their whistles at us to stop. They reached the edge of the parking lot which was directly below the hill on which we were standing. The leader of the fivesome said matter-of-factly via a megaphone, "You men are asked to disperse quietly. Snowball fights are against university policy and you must stop throwing them immediately. If you do not disperse quietly and return to your dorms in an orderly fashion, we will be forced to take punitive actions against you."

Mistake Number One: There were only five of them. Mistake Number Two: They didn't know what kind of demented minds they were dealing with in Jakey and Cheeks. Mistake Number Three: They were standing at the bottom of the hill. That's all I have to say. You get the picture.

We stood looking down at them. An eerie twenty seconds of silence passed. Again the leader spoke, more harshly into the megaphone this time, "I am *ordering* you to disperse and return to your dorms quietly," he barked. Another fifteen seconds of tense silence filled the air.

Then it happened. As if it had been choreographed and practiced beforehand, all one hundred guys on that hill stepped forward into one straight line across the top. We saw what was coming. It was the O.K. Corral, and somebody was about to not be O.K. The security guards saw what was coming. I saw the disbelief in their eyes as they widened with impending horror. The silence screamed for a solution.

Cheeks and Jakey started laughing, a maniacal, diabolical, sinister laugh. One hundred and five men knew exactly what was about to take place—but five of them were on the wrong side, happened to be security guards, and were standing at the bottom of the hill. Jakey let out an Apache Indian yell and, all together, every man on that hill yelled in war-like response, then rained a barrage of snowballs down on those five poor security guards. We pummeled them. When the barrage came to an abrupt halt after twenty of the longest seconds of their lives, chaos ensued as everyone sprinted for their dorms. It was now every man for himself. The guards frantically tried to grab whomever they could. A sea of escapees dashed into every available building door. We ran to EMR's lobby, all of us with our adrenaline pumping and slapping each other high fives for making it back safely. It was a feeling I'll never forget. Jay, Jakey, Cheeks and I laughed for fifteen minutes. I was glad to be a part of it, just another one of too many crazy predicaments that I got into with Jay, Jakey, and Cheeks.

I'll never forget when Cheeks and Jakey "borrowed" a campus security golf cart. They came riding up to the baseball field after practice in the cart they had stolen from in front of the security building. They offered me a ride to the gym and I climbed aboard.

"Where'd you guys get this cart?" I asked, thinking I already knew.

"At the Honda dealer on 67th and Harvard," Cheeks said.

Jakey laughed. "Cheeks, don't lie to Petro. We got it from the Pontiac dealer on 31st and Sheridan."

"You guys are some sick puppies," I chuckled.

"Don't forget to tip your drivers," quipped Cheeks.

Unbeknownst to me, campus security guards were combing the campus in other carts looking for them. Thirty seconds after they dropped me off at the gym entrance, I saw the abandoned security golf cart rolling by itself down the sidewalk at the bottom of the hill. Jakey and Cheeks ran frantically by me into the gym, guards in hot pursuit. "Hey, come back here, you two!" the guards yelled. Jakey and Cheeks never got caught. Figures.

During my freshman year I tried out for the nationally ranked ORU Titan baseball team. They were coming off their first ever visit to the College World Series. After several months of workouts, I was let go—cut—dissed— heartbroken—disappointed because I could have gone to many other colleges and played, but ORU was where I felt called and wanted to be. Mike Moore, our ace pitcher, was eventually drafted by the Seattle Mariners in the 1981 draft. He was not only a first-round draft choice, but was the first player taken overall—of anybody! He ended up spending fourteen years in the majors with the Mariners, A's and Tigers. I eventually played with other future major leaguers like Keith Miller, Kelvin Torve, and Tom Nieto.

I worked hard getting in shape the summer before my second year in school as I prepared to try out for the Titans again. Larry Cochell, the head coach, heard that I was Rico Petrocelli's nephew and wanted to see what I could do. He worked with me, but I didn't make the final cut. I was close—I was *this* close. At least I made an impression on him—that made me feel better. Still, any athlete is not satisfied with almost doing something. They have to *do* it.

The next summer I was determined to come back faster, stronger, and with a better batting stroke. At six feet two inches and 180 pounds, I felt better prepared to succeed this time. I do believe that you can not only prepare to succeed but you can prepare to fail. I worked hard all summer in Brooklyn and felt that this was my time to shine.

It was a gorgeous late August day in Brooklyn when I tore up my ankle. The days were still warm, but the nights were cooling down—a great time of the year. Just days before heading back to school for the fall semester, I was just about to finish up a good thirty-minute bike ride. My legs felt strong. They were tired, but it was a good tired. I was cooling down and heading for the homestretch of my ride, just a few blocks from my house, when I rode too close to a curb. My pedal caught and pulled my ankle under with it. Down I went. Ligaments tore.

I was devastated. I had worked all summer long, determined to make the Titans. I wanted to make my father and Uncle Rico proud. Now, after a stupid bicycle accident, I could hardly walk, let alone be in any condition to make the team.

On the floor of the ORU's basketball arena are the words "Expect a Miracle." I knew that if I were to make the team now, I would truly have to believe for a miracle. I believed in that phrase. I needed a miracle desperately. Back at school during the tryout, some friends came to the stadium to encourage me on. I knew I would have to put the adversity behind me and think about the goal I wanted to achieve. My defense and my arm strength have always been solid, but hitting is what makes or breaks you in baseball. I stepped up to the plate for the first pitch from Jim Brewer, the assistant coach who used to pitch for the Dodgers and Angels (I ended up having a lot of Three Stooge fun with Coach Brewer.) All I wanted to do was to make good contact with the ball each time.

The first pitch screamed by. It was a perfect strike. I saw it go by right down the pipe. I stepped out of the box and dug my feet in to get comfortable. The next pitch came in and I fouled it off, hard down the first base line.

"I'm swinging late," I said to myself. "Get this pitch, now. Get this pitch." The next four pitches I hit hard for clean base hits. I felt good about it. I got into a groove and the bat felt sweet and smooth. Coach Cochell took a liking to me and saw potential in me as a player. My hard work had, in fact, paid off, as I made the team both my junior and senior years. I was a Titan. I had done it, but not without a fight. We were again ranked in the Top Twenty both years that I played, and just missed going to the College World Series. During part of the season we were ranked Number One in the nation. Oklahoma State beat us by one run two years in a row. These were bitter defeats, especially because there was such an intense rivalry between the two schools. Nonetheless, it was a tremendous experience to play with and against some of the guys I played with. Roger Clemens of the Red Sox was pitching for Texas, along with Spike Owen. Kevin McReynolds, now with the New York Mets, played at the University of Arkansas.

J.L. Johnson Stadium, our ballpark, was one of the most beautiful college fields in the country. I remember how proud I was at being able to put on the uniform and play in such a great facility. It was a tremendous opportunity, but I was used sparingly as a substitute outfielder. I had excellent speed and a good arm, but for some reason I couldn't hit the curve ball. I joke about it today that there were only three things keeping me from a lucrative pro career: Fouled off the fast ball, fouled off the change-up, but couldn't touch the curve ball.

All four years at ORU I lived in the "middle-class" dorm, E.M. Roberts Hall. About six hundred guys lived there, about thirty-six on each wing. They were all regular, down-to-earth guys from all over the country, and even international students from Kenya, Hong Kong, Canada, Nigeria, Iran—everywhere. The richer, preppy students lived in the Towers, which were nicer and cost more. There definitely was a separation of classes. I could have lived with the athletes in the athletic dorm, but I decided I'd rather stay in EMR so that I could have the best of both worlds. One thing I did take advantage of was eating at the AD. They had their own cafeteria and the food was better than in the main cafeteria. No matter what dorm you were in each had a set of guidelines.

Every Monday night at 11 p.m. every floor on campus had a mandatory "wing meeting." All thirty-six guys sat out in the hall together on the floor and the resident advisor made announcements, gave sports results from intra-murals, scheduled events, sister-wing activities, and so on. It was a great time to get together and sit around and laugh and joke. Wing meetings were supposed to last about twenty minutes, but we had so much fun that we'd often go on for thirty or forty-five minutes. The term now used to describe what happened at wing meetings is "male bonding," but it was actually more than that. These were good, solid guys, a bunch of guys who really cared about each other and how each one felt. The feeling was sincere and it was genuine. It transcended where we were raised and where we came from. We knew where we were going. We were headed for the same goal—a much higher goal.

All thirty-six of us sat on the floor of our long hallway on our Youngblood Wing. Riv took a moment to count heads. "Who's missing? Anybody?"

"We're all here, Riv," Dietmar Krein said.

"All right, let's get started with a word of prayer. 'Dear Father God, we thank You for this group of men on Youngblood. We ask that You would be in our midst now as we talk and fellowship together. Go before us in all we do this week—in our studies and what we do for You. Help us to glorify You in what we say and do. In Christ's name. Amen.'"

Everybody echoed, "Amen."

"Now the first thing we have to talk about is that this week is Secret Sister week," Riv said.

A voice from the back said, "I don't have any money. I'd hate to have me for a secret brother, poor as I am."

"Do like Petro did last year and give her a can of string beans one day, and a can of baked beans the next day!" another voice proclaimed.

Everybody laughed. "And, Pet, don't sign 'Love, your Secret Brother— Bobby Petrocelli' this time, either," another voice chimed. There was a huge roar this time. It was one of those moments that we laughed because it was funny—and we laughed because it was true. The previous year I had given a signed card on the second night, "Love, Your Secret Brother—Bobby Petrocelli."

The phone rang in someone's room. "That's the sisters calling to say, 'No green or baked beans this year, please!'"

Everybody was always cutting up and joking all the time. The one time during the wing meeting that we never joked around was during prayer. We sincerely lifted each other up in prayer concerning anything that someone wanted to share with the group. This was the best time of the meeting because guys would just open up their hearts and speak freely and honestly about family concerns or prayer requests. Yeah, we knew how to joke, but we also knew how to care for each other enough to pray for one another.

I look back now and it's amazing to me how it was planned out. There's no doubt in my mind that every step of the way of my being at ORU was part of a larger, complex, yet complete plan that was being orchestrated for me, from the guys I met on my wing, to my making the baseball team—even after the bicycle accident. It was as if a blueprint for action were already in motion on my behalf.

Texas Belle

I t was the beginning of my senior year when I first met Texas belle, Ava Dorsett. I had just come off of an awesome summer. I had worked for Richie Donato in Brighton Beach Brooklyn at his produce street stand. Jay and I would unload trucks, stack the stand and clean up. We met so many Brooklyn "characters." It was a time that I helped many of those who were distraught. Little did I know my experience of working with Richie would even prepare me to meet Ava. Little would I know, twenty years later, Richie would be working with me. That summer began a lifelong friendship with him.

Ava was standing on the steps of the cafeteria talking with Jay and her best friend, Toni Swain, whom Jay was dating. Toni was a tow-headed blonde, the type of girl who turned heads when she entered the room, but my head turned toward Ava. Ava had beautiful, long, brown hair, an angelic face, and dimples that deepened when she smiled. I acted like I always did when I met an attractive girl for the first time—excited, constantly smiling or trying to suppress the smile on my face, and trying to come across as a pleasant guy with a good sense of humor.

"Hey, Bobby," Jay said. "I'd like you to meet Toni's friend, Ava Dorsett."

"Hi, Bobby, it's nice to meet you," she said in a soft Texas accent that made my name sound gently like *Bawby*. "Jay has talked a lot about you."

"Don't believe a word he says. I'm not Travolta's brother," I joked. She smiled and gave a cute little giggle.

She got the joke, I thought to myself. This was good. Sometimes a girl I joked with thought I was serious and I'd feel stupid. But Ava got it. A good sense of humor, I thought.

"Jay says you're a P.E. major?"

"Yes. Health and phys ed. I'd like to teach and coach."

"Oh, really?" she said. "My parents are both former physical education teachers. They loved it."

We talked about ten minutes more. I found out that her parents were not only former P.E. teachers, but coaches as well. Ava's father had gone to the University of Houston and played in the NFL for the Oakland Raiders and the Houston Oilers before they became the Texans.

Our relationship was not a "love at first sight" type of thing, but we spent time together with Jay and Toni and gradually developed a friendship that deepened as the days went by. During the first three months, we got to know each other through going out in groups or with other couples. Jay, Toni, Ava, and I spent a lot of time together. The four of us ate together, studied together, and went to the movies together. Mazzio's Pizza (nothing like my New York favorites) was a popular gathering spot for the four of us.

I liked Ava because she was fun to be with and because she liked a lot of the same things that I did. We took study breaks, usually twenty minutes or so, and read the Bible together. We worked in community outreach programs together. We had a compatibility, a kind of chemistry. Our desire to serve God and others was at the center of our lives. We both understood the fundamentals of life's simple things. I felt comfortable with her and, above all, I felt a freedom to be myself. I continually realize how important that is for all of us.

That's something that I would always look for in a woman: if she was cool in letting me be myself. "Hiya, toots," I'd say in my high-pitched Curly voice from "The Three Stooges." "Oh, a wise guy, eh? I'll show you. Ladee ladoo, nyuck nyuck nyuck, whoop oop oop oop oop." I continued through the whole routine. I like to joke around and be silly and goofy sometimes. Other times I like to be serious. I just wanted to be able to be real with whomever I dated. That was important to me. That's something young people should look for: someone they can be themselves with and not feel as if they have to be something they're not.

I remember spending the entire day at beautiful Keystone Lake State Park outside of Tulsa with Jay, Toni (spelled this way because she is not Italian), and Ava. It was a beautiful park with a big lake and trees all around, a place to take a welcome break from being around school on a Saturday. It was a gorgeous day—sunny, warm, and with blue skies. The water on Lake Keystone was a deep, rich, royal blue. There was a crispness in the air, a bite—clean and refreshing like a spring day. It was one of those magical days that you wish you could bottle up and bring out whenever you want to. They only happen about once a year and you have to make sure you take advantage of them when the opportunity arises.

This reminded me of being at Nanny and Beepa's house in the Catskill Mountains. Always in the summertime, though. Late summer. August. The morning would be cool and breezy, then by midday it would be warm enough to swim. And at night just after the sun went down, the crickets would sing. Nanny would make sure we put on a sweater if we went outside in the cool night air. This was a Nanny and Beepa night. "*Bob*-by, come *here*. Put dis sweater on, it's chilly outside," Nanny would say, right before she broke into Norwegian, playfully scolding Beepa for not getting a sweater for me himself.

I can still smell that musty old sweater and the scent of the woods, and the unmistakable fragrance of pine all around me. Every once in a while I'll get that feeling of *déjà vu*—a certain aroma, a familiar face, or just something that reminds me of something from the past. I like it when that happens. It touches places in my heart that I thought I had forgotten. I like to remember. I miss Nanny and Beepa. I also miss going to the mountains—places from a more innocent, simple, unsophisticated time.

That night at the lake, after three months of friendship, I finally decided that Ava was someone with whom I'd like to have a more serious relationship. I had met Ava for the first time around the last week of August, and it was now October. As hard as it may be to believe, I was about to kiss her for the very first time. I was old-fashioned that way.

The sun had set about an hour and a half earlier. It was a spectacular setting—long, warm, full of reds, oranges, and yellows. We sat there for the entire eleven minutes that it took the sun to completely fade from the sky. The silhouettes of the trees all around the park were mysterious and spooky, yet there was a natural, haunting beauty that enveloped us for a half hour more as the light faded into the darkness of night. It had been another wonderful touch to an already terrific and memorable day. But the night was still young, and there was romance in the air.

"Today has been as close to perfect as I could ever ask for," Ava said softly, in her slight Texan accent.

"Yep," I said, "we picked an awesome day to come out here."

We had made a fire and the embers were glowing an almost inviting red-orange. There's something mesmerizing about staring into the glowing coals and embers of a fire. You look at them and stare, almost as if you're in a stupor, captured in their trance-like power. The crickets had begun their songs, the fireflies were dancing an enchanting ballet of lights around us, and the crackle of the wood in the fire was the only thing that brought me out of my sleep-like stare. I don't know if this is true for everyone, but for me it is: I'd get to the point in a relationship in which we hadn't yet kissed, and know I was facing the moment of truth. It could be a couple weeks, a month or, in this case, three months.

Over the last few weeks, I had gotten comfortable with Ava and was wondering when the right time would be—the right time to kiss her for the first time. She sighed a heavy sigh as we both were transfixed by the amber coals in the fire. She shifted her position and snuggled closer to me, so that we were touching side-to-side, shoulder-to-shoulder, hip-to-hip. She leaned into me and rested her head on my shoulder. I looked over at her and she smiled that patented Ava smile, the one where her top lip got thin, she showed her perfect white teeth, and her dimples deepened on her cheeks.

I looked at her smile, then looked into her eyes. I could feel my heart start to beat faster and I breathed short, awkward breaths of air. She reached over and touched the back of my hand with hers and I got goose bumps in an instant. We both looked in each other's eyes and started to lean in toward one another's space. Slowly, slowly, we merged and melted into each other's "personal space" zones—that intimate space that only a few selected people in our lifetime are permitted to enter. I saw her eyes close right before I closed mine, and then felt her soft, moist lips lock with mine. The first touch turned into a deep, meaningful, passionate kiss, one I'll never forget—my first one with Ava, that October night in Keystone State Park near Tulsa, Oklahoma. Today, a lot of people consider it an insult to *not* get a kiss on the first date. Some people expect more. This was the beginning of what I hoped would be a long and deepening relationship. Over the next several months, I found out that Ava wanted this as much as I did—a long and deepening relationship.

During Christmas break in 1981, Ava asked me if I wanted to fly down to Friendswood, Texas, near Houston, to meet her family. Usually when you get to the point of meeting someone's family—especially if she's flying you down from New York to Texas—you think something is happening. Something *was* happening. For the first time, my parents saw that I was serious about this girl being the one with whom I wanted to spend my life.

"Ma," I said from the living room, yelling into the kitchen, "I'm gonna go back earlier than I'd planned from Christmas break."

"You're going back to school early, Bobby?" she asked, puzzled. "My cooking not good enough for you anymore?"

"No, Ma. It's not your cooking. You're the one-and-only Greta the Great when it comes to cooking. You know that, Ma," I joked.

"You don't like your Christmas presents?" she said with a New York snap in her voice.

"No, no, no, Ma. Would you let me finish what I'm trying to say? I'm flying down to Houston to meet Ava's parents—and then drive back to Tulsa with her."

This surprised my mother. She stood speechless for a few seconds, trying to comprehend what I had just told her. Before this, I don't think my mother or my father had given much thought to the fact that I actually liked Ava as much as I did—probably because she was from Texas—well, mostly because she was from Texas. I had never thought I would think seriously about marrying someone from Texas, either. I wasn't opposed to it, but if you had asked me at any time before I met Ava if I thought I would marry someone from the Lone Star State, I would have laughed. Ava and I were from two different worlds. I knew how Texans joked about New Yorkers. And I also knew how New Yorkers joked about Texans. It cut both ways.

I was excited and scared about going to meeting Ava's parents—and their first impressions of me. Meeting a girlfriend's family is always nerve-racking. On the plane ride to Houston I kept thinking, Will her father like me? Will her mother think I'm good enough for her daughter? What if I come across as a schlem? If they don't like me, will I still be able to date their daughter? Will they make fun of my Brooklyn accent? Will my manners be good enough? Can I be myself around them like I am with her? Will they make me wear a cowboy hat? And boots? Yeeeha! The Brooklyn cowboy! Will I actually see people "moseying along?" I put on the cowboy hat and boots, but no way will I get a belt with my name on the back of it.

As I walked toward the front door of Ava's house, a million thoughts were going through my head. All I wanted to do was make a good impression and not make her parents wonder what Ava saw in me.

"Momma, Daddy, this is *Bawby*," Ava said to her parents with a smile and a confident manner in her tone. The way she introduced me put me at ease. She was so proud and confident that I lost my fears right there.

"Mr. and Mrs. Dorsett, it's a pleasure to meet you, sir, ma'am," I said as I firmly shook both of their hands.

They were both very cordial, but I could tell by the look on their faces after Ava so confidently introduced me that they realized for the first time—just as my parents had—that Ava and I were serious about each other.

"Bobby, it's a pleasure to meet *you*," Mr. Dorsett said in his deep, Texas-accented voice.

"Randall and I have heard so much about you, Bobby," Mrs. Dorsett said in her charming Houston accent. I knew then where Ava got her sweetness and charm—from her mother, Linda.

We made an unlikely match, Ava and me, but we both felt good about it. Mr. D. was an ex-football player and also a well-known high-school football coach in the Houston area. He and his family had ventured into business together to open a concrete plant. Many of his family members worked there. Ava's mother was now at home with Ava's younger sister Randa and volunteered at her church with various women's organizations.

The time with her family went better than I could have anticipated. Mr. and Mrs. D. were wonderfully nice, and they didn't wear cowboy boots or hats. And since they were both former physical education teachers and coaches, we immediately shared a common bond.

During my last semester at school, I carried eighteen credit hours plus three teaching assistantships, which was a heavy load. On a typical day I got up at 6:00 a.m., went to class and taught at my assistantships until 1:30 or 2:00 in the afternoon, sometimes later, went to baseball practice at about 2:00 until 6:00 or 7:00 at night, had dinner at the athletic dorm, and studied until midnight or so before going to bed to look forward to another day just like that one. From the time I got up, it was run-run-run all day until I fell in the bed, exhausted, eighteen hours and several miles of walking later.

With a maximum load of course work, teaching, and winter workouts for baseball, I didn't have time for much else except trying to spend at least some time with Ava. She understood that I was overloaded. Her support during this time made our relationship all the more special.

"You look tired, Bobby. Let me rub your neck, okay?" were some of the best words that I could've heard from Ava on those evenings that we studied together. Almost as good were, "How's my baby, tonight. Tired?" And then she would kiss me on the forehead. She knew that I had been running all day and that I was under pressure to finish school on time and try and keep up with baseball and all.

It's amazing how, when I got into the routine of having eighteen- and nineteen-hour days, every minute was scheduled and there was little wasted time. I learned to focus and narrow my priorities down to what really mattered, a very different mindset than when I had come into school as a freshman fours years earlier. If you compare freshman conversations with those of seniors, there's a stark contrast. It's a shift from, "How's my hair looking?" to "On my résumé— do employers really care about how many activity clubs I've been involved with these past four years?" Seniors know that the party's over and the real world is coming, sometimes faster than they'd like it to.

Still in the role of a back-up outfielder, I could now see more clearly than ever that my baseball career was not going to extend into the major leagues. I had another year of eligibility, but I knew my playing time wouldn't increase with all the top-notch current players and also the blue-chip prospects coming in that fall. Even though I was told that I could play and star at most top collegiate programs in the country, I would not get the playing time I really wanted. In not pursuing my last year of eligibility, I was accepting the fact that I hadn't yet reached my potential in baseball and maybe would not by the time I graduated.

In some ways, I'll have to admit, baseball had taken a backseat to another, more powerful love in my life. It was difficult at first to accept that my pro baseball dream was over, but Ava helped to make it easier. After all, she was the more powerful love in my life.

"Ava, I think I'm finished with baseball," I told her with regret in my heart and a lump in my throat. I was finally admitting that I was good but maybe not on the level to play pro ball. This was a hard thing for me to admit to myself especially after seeing Uncle Rico become a star in the majors.

"You have another year of eligibility. Why don't you think about it?" she said. "You've always dreamed of playing in the majors. You could play minor league ball for a few years and after a while you'd be up in the majors before you knew it."

I sat quietly for about ten seconds and then glanced at her briefly. I then spoke straight down to the floor. "What if I wasn't meant to play professionally? What if I were supposed to play college ball and that's it? Maybe that's something I'll have to accept. I dunno, what do you think?"

She looked at me for a few moments, then walked over to me and put her arms around me, kissed me on the lips, and said, "Bobby, God gave you talent in baseball. He also gave you talent in coaching and many other areas of your life. Who's to say that you won't play baseball again? If we 'Seek first the kingdom of God, and His righteousness, then all these things will be added unto you.'—and that includes baseball. So if your baseball career is over, then you've given God the best games of your life. That's all He asks— that we give our best to Him, so that He can give His best to us."

She was special. She had an insight and a strength that sometimes made me want to cry. She knew what to say and when to say it. To me it's a gift— a divine gift from God. She was my gift from Him—and an awesome one at that.

With thoughts of pro ball behind me, I now planned on moving to Texas after graduation to be near Ava. I had already contacted schools in the Friendswood area about doing my student teaching, which was all I had left to do to complete my teaching requirements. My degree was a bachelor's of science in health and physical education. I loved young people and recognized that I enjoyed coaching more and more because of the impact I could have on their lives in a positive, rewarding way. Shaping young people's lives through education and sports was to become essential to me. It was fulfilling in every sense of the word and also was one of my heart's deepest desires.

After I took my last final exam at ORU, I went back to the dorm and sat quietly by myself, stunned. It seemed just yesterday that I had been a peanut-head freshman, registering for my first class, getting lost, feeling homesick for Sheepshead Bay, and then... BAM! My parents were coming down from New York in a few days to watch me graduate. *Where did the time go? Was I really here for four years? Was this a dream?* I looked at my closet and saw my cap and gown. That was all I needed to see.

I didn't have much time to reflect on what I'd done during my time in Tulsa. It was a blur. I had too many other things to try and wrap up between then and the graduation ceremony. My family was coming to Tulsa. Ava's family was coming to Tulsa. The Petrocellis meeting the Dorsetts. The Dorsetts meeting the Petrocellis. New York meeting Texas. I had no idea what was going to happen. What would my parents think? What would Ava's parents think? Would my father wear a cowboy hat? There's no way Greta would put on boots. Attilio, the urban cowboy? Greta the cowgirl? I don't think so. Not in this lifetime. But I know a lot of people who would pay good money to see that.

It was a stressful time for me. So much was happening at once with trying to close out the school year—I was finishing assistantships and moving all my stuff and saying goodbye to all my friends with whom I had lived for four years. And on top of that, my parents and Ava's parents were going to meet for the first time. Ava had every confidence in the world that it would be fine, and she was right. Mr. D. wasn't able to come because of work, but my parents met Mrs. D., Randa, and Ava's grandmother, Meemaw.

"Mom. Dad. I'd like you to meet Ava's mother, Linda Dorsett, her Grandmother, Meemaw And this is Ava's sister Randa." It was a little awkward, nonetheless. Mr. D. wasn't there, for one. Also, my parents are Brooklyn to a T, and they were still not completely convinced that I knew what I was doing in the love and dating department. And then, even though they were all adults, I knew they too were feeling some uneasiness and anxiety. We as young people need to give adults more credit. All four of them knew that what Ava and I had was real—for keeps.

I was so happy when that day was over.

Sadly, I wasn't able to properly say goodbye to my friends and teachers. Maybe you never do. Maybe because you can't. After four of the most difficult yet exhilarating years of our lives together, there's no way to fully express in one minute the depths of our feelings while shaking hands and introducing them to family, then moving on to the next person you must say goodbye to.

"Congratulations, Bobby!" Rob said as he shook my hand, wearing his cap and gown just as I was.

"Thanks. Mom and Dad, this is Rob Knitt, a good buddy of mine from Wisconsin. We were on Youngblood together."

A few seconds later, "Petro, congratulations, man. Hey, I want you to meet my parents. They're here from Montana… "

"Joe, I'll talk to you later, buddy," I said as he walked away. But you never get to talk to them later. There is no later. Later turns into never. That's how it goes. That's the reality of it. We're here one day. Gone the next. Just like my four years at ORU.

Following graduation, I moved to Texas. Ava and I both felt strongly that we had a future together. School was over. That chapter in my life was now history. A new and exciting chapter, with Ava and my teaching and coaching career, was about to begin. I couldn't have been happier.

Full of Dreams

If I had thought Tulsa was hot, then Texas was Saudi Arabia hot. I was jumping out of the frying pan into the fire. This was heat I never knew before. You can truly cut the humidity in Houston with a chainsaw. Fresh out of college, I first worked as a "yard boy" at the Dorsett Brothers Concrete Plant in Pasadena, Texas. That summer and fall of 1982, I cleaned and swept the offices, hosed down the trucks and floors, and greased the machinery, valves, fittings, and conveyor belt that carried the ingredients to make the concrete.

It was a dirty, grimy job and I didn't enjoy it to say the least. It was humbling after just finishing my college degree. This is not what I worked hard to get through college for. Most of the people in the plant were not, let's say, "sympathetic" toward New Yorkers, and I had to constantly put up with their comments and derogatory jokes about people from New York. This made it tough to look forward to work every day but, on the other hand, I had a job, for which I was grateful. Though I did enjoy working with Ava's relatives—especially her cousin B.J. He made my time at the plant more tolerable and even enjoyable at times. We spent much time talking about life as it related to faith issues. Even though I was a college graduate, I came from a hard-working, blue-collar background, but this was not what I wanted to do for the rest of my life. This was not my calling, but it was part of my life's process—learning that life is not a destination, but a journey. I would work at the concrete plant for about nine months, but my heart longed to be working with youth.

By the spring of 1983, I was doing what I loved—working with kids. I began my student teaching in nearby Friendswood at the elementary, junior high, and senior high schools. Ava had finished her senior year of high school at Friendswood. In addition to teaching, I volunteered as a coach, assisting the varsity coach in off-season football and baseball. We did light workouts consisting of running, weight training, and stretching. This was such a positive and welcome change for me. I was doing something that I loved to do—coaching kids.

Pearland, where I lived, and Friendswood are suburban areas just south of Houston and not far from the beaches of Galveston—not a bad place to settle down and raise a family, I thought as I became familiar with the area—beautiful homes, plenty of land and open space, spread out, and a comfortable environment. Things were big in Texas. It reminded me of some places in Tulsa. It had a similar feel.

Ava was finishing her psychology degree at the University of Houston–Clear Lake while working at the concrete plant, keeping books and doing clerical work. Somehow she still found time to volunteer at a women's shelter called "The Bridge." She absolutely loved it. Ava was a people person—very compassionate and sincere in counseling women who had come from broken and abusive marriages and working with unwed pregnant girls, alcoholics, and drug addicts.

Ava lived at home with her parents. They had a beautiful place in Friendswood with a pool, Jacuzzi, gorgeously kept gardens, and a nice piece of land—a nice place to enjoy after work because, to me, it was like going to a spa—a relaxing, luxurious spa.

The best friendships are those in which there is a balance in giving and taking. Problems can easily arise when one person is giving too much, and the other person is taking too much. Ava and I had a good balance of give and take. Ava always tried to show me with her actions that she cared for me. This made her that much more attractive—knowing that at times she was putting me before herself. I reciprocated. That's what love does—it reciprocates. It reflects good things back to the person who sends good things. It makes you care that much more—knowing that someone really cares and wants the best for *you*. *Little did she know what I had planned for us.* So, on October 1, 1982, I took Ava out to a posh, classy restaurant. Our waiter started us with jumbo shrimp cocktails and garden fresh salad *du jour*. I guess they served different specialty salads every day. Next came the house soup that was absolutely out of this world, then lemon to refresh our palates, and we couldn't wait for the main course. I ordered filet mignon and she had lobster tail *a la supremeta*. I had absolutely no idea what a *la supremeta* was, but I was happy that Ava ordered it so I could finish what she couldn't. I could have steak *and* seafood. It was going to be a good night.

After more lemon to clean and refresh our palates and a dessert of cheesecake raspberria and chocolate mousse, Ava and I took a stroll in the gardens behind the restaurant. We strolled by a gazebo surrounded by exotic and seldom-seen flowers, and alongside a stream flowing gently through the garden. We sat outside in the cool breeze and talked about the evening and how much we had enjoyed the meal and spending a night out together.

It was dusk by now and the sun was just beginning to set. I stepped away from the wooden bench that we were sitting on, got down on one knee, and held her hand in mine.

"Ava Dorsett, do you think you wouldn't mind marrying me very much?" It was a line I had stolen from the original *Rocky* movie, in which Rocky asks

Adrienne to marry him with the same quirky words. "What are you doing for the next, ahhh, fifty years or so," he says. "Do you think you wouldn't mind marrying me very much?"

After I said these words, Ava looked deep into my eyes and I could see the tears starting to form.

"Yes, Bobby Petrocelli," she said. "I would love to marry you." My proposal came exactly on our one-year anniversary of our first date. We planned a spring wedding to coincide with spring break at ORU so our friends there could come. The date was set for March. Anybody who's ever had to plan a wedding will tell you that it's a tremendous amount of work. They also say to start early because there are always details that you may forget. You learn a lot about your future mate in planning the event.

I'm a very detail-oriented person, and so was Ava. We complemented each other well and had all the bases covered: guest list, flowers, the wedding program, a photographer, the reception, honeymoon plans—everything.

We were married in Friendswood United Methodist Church on March 12, 1983, with seven groomsmen, seven bridesmaids, and about three hundred in attendance. It was a wonderful wedding—a real celebration. Our families were there and our friends and loved ones. The reception was at the Dorsetts' home. This was truly an awesome day, and I was on cloud nineteen.

I hadn't slept very well the night before because I had all of my groomsmen plus my best man sleeping in my apartment together: Jay, Jakey, Riv, Craig Olson, Cheeks, and Bruno. I was glad they didn't have some crazy bachelor's party for me the night before. I was so exhausted I wouldn't have enjoyed it. Instead, after the rehearsal dinner, we had gone back to my apartment and hung out and talked until the wee hours of the morning. That was just what I wanted to do. These were my best friends who were like brothers to me. I just wanted to spend time with them and laugh at some of the crazy and stupid things we had done together over the years.

I was nervous that day because I wanted everything to go well and everyone to have a good time. So much planning had gone into this wedding, I wanted it to be the best we could possibly have. I arrived at the church an hour and fifteen minutes early so that we all could get dressed and relax before the ceremony. As we got dressed in the back choir room of the church, my brother-in-law Nicky couldn't find his bow tie anywhere and started to get panicky. He and Ava's cousin Bill were the only two groomsmen who hadn't stayed with the rest of us in my apartment the night before.

"I'm gonna get your sista," said Nicky in a testy and impatient voice. "I'm gonna get Debbie. She forgot to give me my bow tie. I can't go out there without a bow tie. It looks stupid!" Nicky had already torn up the room looking for the tie but without any luck. Finally, fifteen minutes before the ceremony, he found it hanging on a hanger with the rest of his tuxedo stuff.

When all this was going on, it started to settle in on me what a big plunge this was—to be getting married. I tried not to be hyper, but I didn't do a good job of being calm. I kept moving and pacing, moving and pacing, moving and pacing. I was so happy when the time came, and I could leave that choir room and start walking toward the sanctuary. Down the corridor I walked. In the distance I heard the buzz of excitement coming from the sanctuary. This was it. There was no turning back. Closer, closer, closer we walked. I took a deep breath right outside the side entrance to the front of the sanctuary and prayed a silent prayer, "God, thank You for today—a day I've waited all of my life for. Amen." Then I walked to the front of the sanctuary with Bruno, my best man.

I'll never forget the moment I saw Ava appear in the door wearing her wedding gown. She was stunning—absolutely stunning. I had such a rush of emotion upon seeing her and knowing that she was about to become my wife that I almost cried right there. If I hadn't been completely exhausted from the planning and events leading up to the wedding itself, I would've cried my eyes out. But I didn't. And I'm glad I held back.

She slowly walked toward me and I could see her "Ava smile," the one where her top lip got thin, she showed her perfect white teeth, and her dimples deepened in her cheeks. I couldn't take my eyes off her. She hypnotized me with her radiance and the sheer joy that beamed from her infectious smile.

"Who gives this woman to this man?" the pastor asked.

"Her mother and I," Mr. D. said.

I took Ava's hand. Goose bumps covered me at the mere touch of her skin, and it reminded me of the very first time I had kissed her in Keystone

State Park in Oklahoma. In a few moments I would kiss her again. This time it would be different. This time it would be as Mrs. Robert James Petrocelli.

I couldn't wait for her lips to touch mine. It would be the best kiss since the first, and the sweetest of my life.

That night we stayed in Houston and flew to Acapulco, Mexico, the next morning for what would be an incredible honeymoon. The sun was shining brightly, the sand was white as snow, and the water was crystal clear. I could see all the fish and coral in the Gulf.

"Ava, should we move here?" I joked.

"I've already got the house picked out," she jabbed back at me. "See that grass hut over there?" I laughed, and then she kissed me. "You think I'm kidding, don't you?"

It was a different world. This was paradise. If this were any indication of how our life together would be, then why hadn't we got married sooner? I could live with this. Give me that grass hut over there. No problem at all. We laid on the sun-drenched beach late in the afternoon after a full day of para-sailing and shopping. My baby was right beside me, and she looked both delicious and inviting. As I laid there I peered at Ava through my sunglasses, squinting and smiling at her.

"Bobby, what are you thinking about?" she asked.

"My wife," I said as I gazed at her. It felt good to say those words. *Mrs. Petrocelli*, I thought to myself. *Mrs. Ava Petrocelli. Mrs. Ava Robert Petrocelli. Mrs. Ava Robert James Petrocelli.* This is the one I had been looking for. Mrs. A.R.J.P. It had a ring to it. That was *my* girl. She was mine. She belonged solely to me. And nobody else on this beach could have her. This was one of those moments, a time you can say to yourself, "This is good. This is very good."

America, what a great country. A beautiful wife, and though I wasn't playing baseball, I was beginning a career doing what I love the most, teaching and coaching "yutes."

When I finished student teaching at Friendswood High School, I accepted a full-time position as a health education teacher and coach at Santa Fe High in nearby Alta Loma. Friendswood had no teaching openings but it turned out that Santa Fe was in the same district as Friendswood. It was a great situation. My first position included teaching health education and coaching freshman, JV, varsity football and yeah, varsity baseball. I was the head baseball coach—combining two of my loves—baseball and yutes. My typical day started about 7:00 o'clock each morning and ended between 7:00 and 11:00 p.m.—always the later during football season. Texans take football seriously. Thousands would attend games. Towns would shut down—not like Brooklyn. We would be lucky if twenty came to our games. But our Brooklyn teams were tough. On defense, after we sacked the quarterback, we would go into the stands and sack his family. I learned more about football during my first week of practice than I had known my entire life.

I loved to coach, but more than that I loved the kids. Kids want people who are real in their lives and that was my goal—to be all the things to them that I had even wanted growing up. They hung on my every word as if it were the most important thing in the world. For some reason coaches are looked upon with higher esteem than other teachers and, in many cases, are respected more than parents. It's part of the job. It comes with the territory. It's how our society looks at members of the coaching profession—as mentors, as role models.

"Now listen to me carefully," I would rally them before a game. "I want every one of you to give me everything you've got out on that field today. Try your best—that is all I ask. So win or lose, you will be a champ because you always gave your best. That is how life works. This team has been mouthing off and talking trash all week long that they're gonna kick our butts. It's true—they have better athletes than we do. It's true—they are bigger and stronger than we are. It's also true—they are undefeated up to this point midway through the season."

"But let me tell you something right here and now. If you go out there and play four quarters of hard football like you've been practicing all week, you're not only going to win this game, you're going to stomp this team. And when it's over, I don't want anybody to brag—because winners don't brag. Men don't brag. Winners—and men—shake the other team's hand and say, 'Good game. I enjoyed it.' And when this season's over and you're long gone from Santa Fe High School in Alta Loma, Texas, I want each of you to know this: Nobody remembers the score; nobody remembers who wins and who loses. It's your attitude that's never forgotten." My attitude was to always let them know I am here for them—here to serve them and help them to become all that they are destined to be.

Besides teaching and coaching, I worked as a club sponsor for FCA (Fellowship of Christian Athletes) and SADD (Students Against Destructive Decisions—which used to be called Students Against Drunk Driving). Ava and I also served as youth leaders at Lakewood Church, the most-watched Christian church television program worldwide, hosted by Joel Osteen (author of the *New York Times* best seller, *Your Best Life Now*). I actually went to college at ORU with Joel. Amongst our other duties, we volunteered to help with the Sunday morning program, which included ministering to several hundreds of teens ranging in age from thirteen to eighteen. This was important to us because we both recognized the values that had been instilled into our lives as youngsters growing up in a Christian environment. The group of kids was so large that often we held separate meetings just for the teens.

Ava and I also enjoyed traveling, eating out, spending time with family, and exploring new adventures. Ava's grandmother, Meemaw, had a beach house at Bolivar Island, in Galveston. It was about forty minutes away and was a great getaway. Other times we drove to her house in Kingwood and visited her for a Saturday night and stayed until Sunday. She loved to cook and we loved to eat her cooking. How's that for complementing each other? My grandparents had passed away, but Meemaw always made me feel welcome and at home. "Bobby, how are things with your job?" she'd ask— really wanting to know. She was lovingly involved in the lives of Ava and me—that's the thing I appreciated about her. She really wanted to know the answers to the questions she asked. She wasn't just asking to be asking. She was genuine. I definitely considered her to be MY grandmother. We looked forward to the times we spent with her because visiting her was a nice change of pace from the routine of our everyday lives. Being with Meemaw gave us a different perspective on life—one that I missed with my own grandparents. I think they all would've gotten along together—Nanny, Meemaw, and Beepa. At least, they had great nicknames.

During the first two years of our marriage, we lived in two different apartments. We really wanted a house, but couldn't afford one. Brand-new, more luxurious apartments with cable television and a swimming pool were being completed right across the street from our first apartment. It was a glorious August day when we moved over to The Heights. We only spent four months in our first, smaller apartment.

This was better. It was much cleaner and brighter. Ava and I danced on our carpet in the new apartment. "Burning. Burning. Disco Inferno. Burning. Burning"—I can still hear that music playing. The movie *Saturday Night Fever* was based on my neighborhood in Brooklyn, but Travolta had nothing on me that night. I could've taught him plenty of dance moves. We were finally in a bigger place. *Yessssss!* Goodbye little matchbox. Hello shoe box. This is a part of the intimacy of marriage I love—the excitement of a new home, the holding, the hugging, the snuggling, the "spooning," the warmth, and the simplicity of knowing that my wife is there for me. That's what I like—the knowing. It's a peaceful feeling—a strength and security— that wonderful sense of oneness—two halves making one whole, like pieces to a puzzle fitting together so well—by design. I really felt that with Ava. She saw me when my hair stuck straight up in the air like Don King's. She saw me when I woke up in the morning and my eyes looked like Mr. Magoo's. And she smelled me when I got home from a full day of football practice in the hot sun and I hummed so badly that the neighborhood pets all ran from me when they saw me coming. She knew me at my best; she knew me at my worst; and you know something—she loved me just the same. That's love. That's friendship. That's intimacy. That's marriage.

After two and a half years of apartment living, Ava and I were more than anxious to move into a house. But, with interest rates as high as they were in 1985, we couldn't afford to buy a home just then. The rates were about 9%, not like the 5 1/2% we have now in 2005. Instead, we found a four-bedroom house that we could rent in a brand new housing development in League City at 501 Landing Boulevard. That was our first home. We moved into our house on Labor Day weekend, and were thrilled to be in a place more private—more our own. Who knows? Maybe one day we can own it. Excited would be an understatement.

"Baby, I can't believe it. We're really in a house. *Ahhhhhhhhhh!*" she screamed with excitement. "See that. I can even scream and no one upstairs or downstairs will start banging on the walls and yell, 'Hey, shut up down there. Don't you people ever sleep?'

"And you can laugh as loud as you want. You can watch your *Three Stooges* and *Honeymooners* tapes at any time of the day or night and laugh your heart out, and no one will think that you're a demented hyena or something—well, you are that, but at least no one else will think so, honey," she said. A mischievous smile crossed her face.

"Come on," I said, "let's look at the bedrooms. There's four: One for you and three for me. See how generous I am?"

We ran from room to room like kids playing, and I tackled her along the way in each room.

"Ava's trying for the second bedroom. She's got a slight opening, but—*noooo!* She's dragged down at the five-yard line. Oh, what a game-saving tackle by Bobby Pet Butkus of the Bears!"

"No! *Drrrrrrrrrr.* There's a flag on the play," Ava shot back. "Illegal use of the hands."

"What are you talking about? That's *legal*. You're my wife!" I exclaimed, and I tickled her in all the right places: her stomach, her ribs, and her knees.

"*Stop, Bobby. Stop, Bobby. Stop, Bobby. Stop...*" she laughed as I went to work on her mercilessly.

What a beautiful house—four bedrooms, two baths, a living room with a fireplace, a beautiful bay window in the master bedroom, an alarm system, sprinklers, ceiling fans, a wooden deck, and a microwave.

One word described our new house—space. That's what we liked—space. And we had plenty of it, inside and out. I put my drums in one of the extra bedrooms so I could bang away to my heart's content. I'd bang, bang, bang away. You see, I had to make up for all the lost time I couldn't play living in the cramped apartments. It was a good way to relieve stress. At least, for me it was.

Outside we had a big yard, and because it was a new development, we were the very first house you saw when you came into the neighborhood. A large, grassy area more than a quarter-mile long separated our house from the street coming into the complex. We liked the privacy of having no one on the entire right side of us, nothing except this grass field. In fact, it was so big that I practiced chipping golf balls out there. It was kind of like having my own private mini-course. I should have called it Petro's Greens. "Arnold Petro Palmer steps up to the plate. Oh, there's a blooper to left field—it's gonna drop in for a base hit. One run will score and they're waving in the runner from second base. What a soft touch from Petro Palmer. He's going to hit for the cycle today." As a kid, I always dreamed of having my own baseball field—a big, wide-open, green baseball field. This was close enough. This was my "field of dreams." You see in Brooklyn, my front yard was three feet by four feet and my backyard was five by six. Things are bigger in Texas.

The house was solid brick which we really liked—solid, heavy-duty brick. Occasionally, bad storms and tornadoes posed a threat in any part of Texas so the brick made us feel safer than if it were wood. Ava and I talked about waiting for a brick home once we were finally able to afford a house because there's something psychologically satisfying about having brick, too—at least to us there was. It's more of a fortress kind of feel to me. This is my domain— my castle. Nothing can harm us inside these stone walls. We were young, strong, and still invincible.

A house is not a home until it has a woman's special touch. I'd been to many of my buddies' homes who lived by themselves or with other guys. It's not the same as when a woman adds her touch. Ava loved to decorate. She collected porcelain dolls and decorative pillows that she placed on the ledge of the bay window in our bedroom. Each one had a story behind it. She should have written them down—she might have been the next Dr. Seuss. The dolls and pillows would be keepsakes that we'd pass on to our children, our grandchildren, and our great grandchildren. We had it all planned out. There was a lifetime ahead of us—Ava twenty-three; me, twenty-four. We talked about little bambinos in the near future—a bambinette for her, a bambino for me. We were simple people. We just didn't want twins to start off with—maybe later, but not then.

Our bed was right up against the bay window in the master bedroom. We loved seeing the stars at night flickering in the sky before we fell asleep in each other's arms. Talk about a romantic atmosphere—it was wonderful. Sometimes I would lie there at night with my baby and just gaze at the stars.

We joked that there were "stars in our eyes." There were. I would sing, "Hey there. You with the stars in your eyes... " Ava's eyes would glisten in the moonlight. The way the light fell gently onto her face through the bay window sent tingles through me. Sometimes I'd wake up in the middle of a clear starry night and just watch her sleep. Have you ever done that? Watched your spouse sleep?

"Bobby, what are you doing? Are you staring at me again? What is this—some secret fetish of yours, watching me sleep?" she would playfully ask.

"No, baby. I just can't believe how beautiful you look when you sleep,"

"Get real. Beautiful? You wouldn't say that if the lights weren't off and you could see that I'm not wearing any makeup."

Sleep-watching—it's what newlyweds do—part of the romance, I guess. And it never wore off for us. Maybe because I loved her so much. Maybe because I knew she'd do anything for me. When someone is that committed and dedicated to you, you get a strong feeling inside, a longing that makes you think about that person every minute of the day. You may be in the middle of your workday and suddenly that longing will tug at your heart. Only my love can fill that space because she knows me like a book. When I act like "The Coach"—when I act like a kid—when I let my guard down—when I'm the Bobby no one else has seen, she's my safe haven to run to—a shelter from the storms of life—a refuge in times of discouragement.

Full moons were the best. The light was so bright you could literally see shadows—shadows and silhouettes. They led to more playful evenings. Understated, soft blue moonbeams danced throughout our bedroom on those nights. There seemed to be a warmth in its rays—warm moonbeams.

"Ava, look at this," I said one night with the enthusiasm of an eight-year-old. I was making shadow animals with my hands as the moon shone through our bedroom window. "Here's a rabbit. How about this one?" I asked as I made a crocodile.

"That's easy, honey. You've got to do better ones," she said softly, half asleep.

"Uh, oh. Here's a roadrunner," I warned as I ran my fingers like a running bird over her back. "The roadrunner's looking for the coyote. Is he here?" I asked, moving my hand to the back of her neck.

"*Yelp!*" she screamed, "Bobby, don't start *tickling meeeeee...* " It was too late. The game had already begun.

When we first moved into the house, my dad was visiting. He was visiting from New York and, because he had had a stroke, he got around by using a wheelchair. I remember him being so proud of my house. He bragged about how beautiful it was. I was glad that he shared this time with us because it was he who had drilled into me the importance of family and of working hard to provide for them. Three weeks with Dad was about the right amount, though. He kept us going . . . and going . . . and going. What can I say? He's Attilio! They broke the mold when they made him.

Dad flew back to Brooklyn, and we got back to just Ava and me. It had been nice to have company, but it was nice to have the house to ourselves again—just the two of us, still feeling like newlyweds after two-and-a-half years of marriage.

CHAPTER

Thursday, October 24, 1985

After a long day, I got home about seven o'clock Wednesday night, October 23, and collapsed in front of the television to wind down from the day. The Kansas City Royals were playing the St. Louis Cardinals in the World Series.

Wednesday was really the only day Ava and I would spend quality time together that week. On Mondays I had class at the University of Houston–Clear Lake where I was working on my master's degree in counseling education. Ava spent Tuesday evening at The Bridge, the women's shelter where she volunteered. Thursday and Friday were dedicated to football during the season.

Here it was the end of October and they were still playing baseball. It gets later and later every year. Now they actually play into November. If Boston had not finally won the World Series after eighty-six years (October, 2004) in four games, the seventh game would have been played during the first few days of November. I had taken the TV outside to the deck because it was a gorgeous evening. I was watching Tom Nieto, a catcher for the Cardinals who had played baseball with me at ORU. It was cool, quiet, and uneventful. Ava came out and watched a little of the game with me. She knew I loved sports, especially this time of year during the World Series.

"Who's winning?" she asked.

"Oh, for cryin' out loud!" I yelled at the TV set. "Now you loaded up the bases. This guy couldn't find the plate with a softball!"

Ava giggled at me because I always talked to the TV when I got mad about how the game was going.

"You want more ice tea?" she asked softly, sliding into my lap.

"I'll get some at the end of the... "

I never finished the sentence. She kissed me with one of her warm, soft kisses and, for an instant, I forgot where I was and that I was watching the game—that's how good it was. She smiled her cute smile, the one where her mouth curled up on the side and I could see her dimples really well. It was Ava's "I did it to you again!" smile. She loved to kiss me mid-sentence so that I couldn't get the words out. It was one of those little games she played, and you know what? I didn't mind one bit—not one little bit.

I don't remember much about the game after that. I finally turned the TV off because the light from the set and the announcer's voice were distracting me from the business at hand—you know what I mean. What can I say? Some things are more important than baseball—that's why they made VCRs.

We both woke about 6:00 a.m. the next morning. It's Thursday, it's football season, and today we have a freshman football game in Wharton. Therefore, I will not be back home till approximately 11:00 p.m. Ava showered and then went into the kitchen for breakfast. I waited until she was finished, then took a shower and got ready myself. After I showered, shaved, and did my hair, I went into the kitchen and sat down to have a bowl of cereal, orange juice, and toast.

"We're almost out of milk, baby," I said, as Ava returned to the bathroom to finish getting ready and touch up.

"I'll pick some up after work, okay?"

"Skim milk, all right, honey?"

"Skim milk, Bobby," she said as if she'd heard it a hundred times. Actually, she had. I finished eating, went back into the bathroom, and brushed my teeth. This was really the only time that we shared the bathroom together.

"I have to go to Wharton today," I said, "so I won't be home until 10:30 or so. Remember, today is Nicholas' birthday. If you have time, can you call Debbie and wish him a 'Happy Birthday' from us?"

"I'll do it when I get home tonight."

"I don't want him to think we forgot about it."

"I'll do it tonight," she assured me as she kissed me on the neck.

I got dressed in my street clothes that day: a shirt, a tie, and a pair of slacks. I didn't need to wear coaching attire because on Thursday mornings I could go in a little bit later—for a short team meeting—instead of a morning practice since we had an early evening game.

Ava and I both left the house around 7:00. We both had to be at work by 7:30. She went her direction to her job at the concrete plant, and I went mine.

This particular Thursday was busier than usual. It was so hectic that I didn't get a chance to call Ava at her work and to at least touch base on how her day was going. Several times I thought I had a minute to call, but every time I started to, somebody yelled for me to do something. We left for Wharton, eighty miles away, and were on the road for a couple of hours. Since there were no cell phones then, I really couldn't reach her until I got back to Santa Fe about 10:30 p.m. I knew Ava would go straight from work to the women's shelter as she always did.

"Get him, get him, *get him!*" I yelled at our defensive line during the thick of the game. I watched as five of our boys converged on their quarterback and sacked him for an eleven-yard loss. "Atta boy, Kevin! That's how you pursue! Let 'em know who you are! You're the boss! Atta baby!" I yelled.

The rest of our players on the sideline roared as the defense again stifled Wharton's high-powered offense. The teams lined up for the next play from scrimmage. "Don't jump! Don't jump! He's trying to pull you off-sides!" I exclaimed as their quarterback barked, "*Hut* one. *Hut* two. *Hut*, hut… *hut!*" Nobody went for it. "*Hut*," he barked again, and the center snapped the ball. Our defensive line sliced through their line like a knife through butter and again gang tackled the quarterback.

Again, a huge roar came from our guys on the sideline. The momentum was ours and we couldn't be stopped. It's a great feeling when that happens for your team—but a sick feeling when you're on the other end. I've been on both sides of momentum swings, so I know what it feels like. Our boys played inspired ball that day. I was proud—really proud. We beat a good team that day—a talented, well-coached team.

When the game was over, we hung around to cheer on the junior varsity team. Gary Causey, our assistant principal at Santa Fe, joined me on the sidelines and we chatted about the game and which boys were playing well and which boys were not. We eventually began to talk about life—and then about God.

"Petro, if God is so good, why do people have problems? Why does God allow people to suffer?" he asked.

I paused for a second as I thought about my answer. He had asked a good question—one that I had to ponder for a moment.

"Well," I finally answered, "sometimes problems occur because people make foolish and stupid choices. We can't blame God for that. It's not His fault. If He didn't give us a free will and the chance to make our own choices, we'd be nothing more than robots, following whatever was programmed into our computers and memory banks. God will never force or control anyone to do anything against their will." The movie, *Bruce Almighty*, with actor Jim Carrey, focuses on that same theme. I know I don't have all the answers, but I felt I answered Gary to the best of my understanding.

We talked more about free will and making correct choices. It was a good conversation because Gary was interested in what I believed and had to say.

We boarded the buses to return to Santa Fe and arrived back at the high school around 10:00 p.m. I hung around until all the kids were picked up and gone. Some nights I'd drive kids home but, fortunately, I didn't have to that night. I left the school parking lot at 10:30 p.m. knowing that I had to be back early the next morning for another team meeting and to take care of any football business that hadn't been finished that night. The next night, Friday, would be busy, too. I was scouting Friendswood. Friday nights for me were consumed with traveling and scouting the varsities next opponent.

I had been going since 6:00 a.m. and was tired as I pulled into my neighborhood. There wasn't a more welcome sight in all the world than our red brick home across my grassy field, Petro's Greens. What a great feeling to be home! I pulled into the driveway, opened up the garage door, parked the car, and walked into the kitchen where Ava greeted me, as she normally did, with a hug and a kiss.

"Are you tired, baby?" she asked as I slumped down into my dining room chair.

"Yep," I said, "but we won today. The boys really played well. Really well! I was proud of them because they played like they wanted to win. That was the key. They wanted to win—instead of trying not to lose."

There was a sparkle in her eye that night as she kissed me a second time. She knew how to give me that look to let me know that I was home but, more importantly, that I was hers. I was safe—free to be myself—whichever mood I was in. At school I was the teacher, I was the coach, and also the encourager. But now, at the end of the day, I was the tired little boy. Imagine that—here I am, six foot two and two hundred pounds, and this little woman gives me a smile that makes me want to cry inside. That's what love does. It breaks you down, chews you up, and spits you out. It makes you human. Anyone who's ever been in love will tell you that it's one of the best feelings in the world—that feeling of oneness, that bonding, that surrender, that comfortable sense of vulnerability.

Men won't admit it, but women make us feel this way. Who really has the power? Who really is the boss? Any man will tell you, it's not us.

Ava was always upbeat and energetic on these late nights. It was a great feeling to come home to a wife who was as happy to see me as I was to see her. We knew we wouldn't be able to spend time together until later on that weekend, on Saturday, perhaps. Ava knew the routine—this was my third season coaching football. On Saturday mornings I'd go back to school and break down game films, so I'd only get to see Ava at about two or three o'clock on Saturday afternoons during the season. It was a long week, and I had to repeat this cycle until November when the season finally ended—so I cherished every moment I was able to spend with Ava during football season. She understood that it was part of my job. She was good that way—she knew what I had to do. There is always sacrifice involved when in a profession like mine. Every coach's wife will tell you that.

I walked into the kitchen and there it was—a big bowl of rigatoni with sauce. It was nice and hot. Ava had great timing—like a sixth sense. They say that after couples have been together for awhile, they develop this inner clock that lets them know what the other is doing. I don't know if it's true, but I do know that Ava's timing was extremely good. And even though she wasn't *Italiano*, she made a mighty mean sauce—a Texas-Sicilian kind of meat sauce—the kind that put so much hair on your chest the barber has to use a lawn mower for a shave and a trim.

"Ava, I think that you have relatives in Palermo and Napoli that you're not telling me about. Your father told me his great grandfather changed his name from Dorsettini to Dorsett when he came to America!"

She laughed and swatted at my shoulder. "You're silly," she said, emphasizing her squeaky Texas drawl to let me know she had no Italian whatsoever in her genes—from any generation. She was pure Texas Belle.

Ava had eaten hours before, so she just sat and talked with me. I was just so happy to be home and to be with my baby that it didn't matter what we talked about. We usually talked about how one another's day had gone—things like that.

"So how were things at The Bridge today?"

"Oh, about the same today. No big flare-ups or arguments this time."

She always sat with me while I ate. Most of the time after getting home late like that, I'd eat and she wouldn't, but she always sat with me. Maybe some people wouldn't consider that a big deal, but I liked that she sat in her chair, with no food, just to be with me. It's a simple thing, I know, but it's an important thing. She conveyed a message to me while she sat and watched me eat: She was saying that she loved me. She didn't have to say the words. I knew it. Her actions spoke volumes about the way she felt.

It was eleven o'clock when I got up from the table. "More, Bobby?" Ava asked.

"No, thanks. I'm packed." She always asked me if I had had enough, and I always said, "I'm packed." I knew she would ask, and she knew how I would respond. It was like an inside joke—a game, a chemistry between us. That made it great.

Ava cleaned up the dishes and I went to take a shower. Showers felt good after days like this. I could rinse the weight of the day off me, and Ava wouldn't kick me out of bed for being all grungy and mealy. She didn't have to say the words. Her actions spoke volumes.

When I finished showering I came back out to the living room where Ava was straightening up. I felt refreshed and relaxed.

"Did the tape record?" I asked her.

"Sure did," she said.

One of my favorite things to do on Thursday nights after the long football day was to watch *The Honeymooners*, which I recorded every week. Let's see what Ralph and Norton are up to. I love *The Honeymooners* as much as *The Three Stooges*—and that's a lot. I could sit for hours on end and watch those two shows. I'd laugh and laugh and laugh. It was the type of show that I could have one of those good, hearty, full-bodied, stomach-hurting laughs that we all need once in a while just to remain sane. I was more than ready for it.

Norton and Ralph were going to be on the *Beat the Clock* show in this episode. They were practicing stunts in Ralph's apartment: rolling eggs down a long trough, catching each one, and putting them in the basket before the eggs broke. Ralph rolled them down and Norton tried to catch them and bring them back up to Ralph.

It was a funny show, all right, but my attention was diverted from the television when Ava sat in my lap.

"I heard they taped these shows in front of a live audience," Ava said.

"Yep. If you watch real closely, you can see them mess up sometimes. The chemistry on this show is phenomenal. They knew each other so well—like they knew what the other person was going to do."

"That's why it's so good," Ava said. She was right. The classic television shows are the ones with casts who worked well together.

"We have chemistry, Bobby," Ava softly whispered in my ear as she nibbled on my lobe. "We have anatomy and physiology, too, don't we, honey?"

I somehow forgot about Ralph, Norton, and Alice on the television. I could watch that tape anytime. I was with my own "honeymooner." We cuddled together in the recliner chair talking more about how her day had gone and how hectic the day had been for both of us.

"Do you think some year you'll stop coaching football, Bobby?" she playfully but earnestly asked me. I knew what she was getting at. It was times like these that I wished I could have collected all those hundreds—no thousands—of hours and cashed them in for more moments like this.

We talked about other things while cuddled together in the recliner. "Did you have a chance to call Debbie and wish Nicholas a Happy Birthday?" I asked with anticipation.

"No… I didn't. I was so busy with everything—one thing after another—that I didn't get a chance to. I'm sorry, Bobby."

"Ava, don't be concerned, we can call tomorrow." It was past 11:00 p.m. and New York is an hour ahead of Texas. I didn't want to call and wake him up. "We can call him in the morning to see if he's gotten the card we sent," I told her.

We talked about my family flying down from Brooklyn to be with us for Thanksgiving. They were all coming: my mom, dad, Debbie and her husband Nicky, Nicholas, and my younger sister, Chrissy. My dad had already purchased the plane tickets, and I was looking forward to the visit. Dad was so excited about returning.

"Do you think they'll like it?" Ava asked, referring to the house.

"If they don't, they can sleep in the yard," I joked back at her. "Of course, they'll like it, baby," I reassured her. "You've done a wonderful job with the house, Ava-la. The last time I talked with them they were ecstatic about coming. A Texas Thanksgiving with a taste of Brooklyn"—maybe a new reality show.

Ava then mentioned about the upcoming weekend. "Bobby can we go Thanksgiving shopping on Saturday. Since your birthday is on Thanksgiving, and your family is coming, I want to make it more special then ever."

"Ava, we haven't even gotten candy for the upcoming trick or treaters."

"Don't worry," Ava replies. "We can pick some up while we're out. Maybe get some Mexican food at Casa Ole. How 'bout seeing a new movie or even seeing *Back to the Future* again?"

"Where do you wanna go? Baybrook or the Galleria?" I asked, referring to popular malls nearby.

"Can we do both?" she asked with a child-like smile of anticipation on her face.

"Whatever you wanna do, baby, that's what we'll do."

She smiled and squinted her eyes with approval that the plan was set. It was the type of moment that I loved because I knew she would look forward to it like a kid anticipating a trip to the candy store. Just knowing that she was excited and happy made me happy as well. We connected at that moment. There's something deeply satisfying in a relationship when you get those rare and sometimes too few and far between moments of connection and bonding. But when it happens—it makes everything worthwhile.

When we finished talking, Ava got up, went to the bathroom to freshen up, and got ready for bed. It was about 11:30. *The Honeymooners* was over. She peeked her head around the corner. "Good night," she said, meaning she was headed for bed and I could stay up if I wanted to.

"Good night," I said. I rewound the tape and turned off the TV and VCR. I went into the kitchen to perform my "before I go to bed" ritual. I checked the oven. It was off. The stove. Off. The microwave. Yep. Refrigerator? Closed. Everything locked up? Garage door. Check. Back door? Good. Front door? Double-locked. That's it. Everything's the way it should be. My security duties were over. I could now go to bed with peace of mind knowing that I hadn't forgotten anything. The king had checked the castle, and the castle was secure. I turned off the lights behind me as I made my way to our bedroom making one final stop in the bathroom to brush my teeth.

Ava was already snuggled comfortably in the bed for about fifteen to twenty minutes. I cuddled up beside her because my side of the bed was still cold. That's another simple pleasure that's easily taken for granted—getting in a bed that has already been warmed for you.

We lay there together. "I think my family's going to love the house, Ava, absolutely love it," I said. She reached over and squeezed my thigh—meaning "Thank you for saying that." I remembered what my dad had said, and how proud he was of me for having the house, and working hard to provide for Ava. I wrapped my arms around her and enveloped her completely as we lay in the "spoon" position.

She kissed me goodnight, then I lay there quietly for several minutes trying to relax and let my mind slow down. I was wound up from the day, and my mind was still racing. I thought about the game: Kevin, who had played a great game on defense; Gary Causey, and what we had talked about—wondering if he was lying in bed with his wife, not being able to sleep because he was thinking about our conversation, too. A few minutes passed—the clock showed 11:34. I looked out the bay window and saw the flickering stars. A full moon—it cast a beautiful glow on the ceiling of our bedroom. Awesome. It's what I look forward to. Forget the romance, I know what's important. I threw up both of my hands and made animal figures on the ceiling.

It was a calm night—a calm night after a hectic day. I was glad the week was almost over. I started to think back about specific plays in our game that afternoon—things that had worked—things that had not. For some reason, I always second-guess the day's events at night when I'm lying quietly in bed. Maybe it's natural—for me it was. I liked this part of the day because it was a time to reflect, pray, and unwind—let my mind rest after racing for the entire day.

Five more minutes passed and I still couldn't sleep. I looked out again at the stars and moon. *It's a vast universe*, I thought. *All the stars and planets out there. Four billion people in the world and God loves each one of us. Yes, indeed. He had given me a good life. I love the kids at Santa Fe. Love Ava—I have a good woman. Love my house. My family (A La Familia). My friends, and most of all, my God. What more could I ask for?* I had been truly blessed.

The clock now showed 11:40. I got out of bed and stumbled through the dark to the kitchen to get a glass of milk. Milk helped me sleep. It settled me down. I would wake up with sour breath the next morning, but that's the breaks. I opened the refrigerator and found that the carton was empty, so I had a glass of water instead.

When I came back to bed, I mentioned to Ava that there was no milk. Half asleep, she mumbled, "I'll get some first thing in the morning." I touched her on her side to say that I appreciated her doing that. I said a few prayers out loud for the two of us. I liked to do that before we went to sleep. This was important to me—starting the day with prayer and ending the day with prayer. You have to do things right.

"God, thank You for today and for being with us during our trip to Wharton for the game. Thank You for keeping us from any injuries. I pray that You will be with each of the kids and other coaches as they sleep tonight. Give them a deep, restful sleep. I pray that tomorrow will be a good day and that we'll be able to accomplish all that You have for us to do. Be with our families tonight, and keep them safe. Thank You for being with Ava at her job and in her work at the women's shelter. I pray that You will continue to use her there, to bless the ladies and girls who are going through so much adversity and difficulty in their lives. Give us a restful and deep sleep this evening. We pray all these things in Your name. Amen."

Ava mumbled, "Amen." I kissed her on the cheek and turned over to go to sleep. It was now between 11:40 and 11:45. It had been a good day—a full day. I had accomplished a lot that day, and had many things to be proud of, but now it was time to sleep—a time to relax—a time to let the cares of the day just drift into oblivion. I lay there quietly for a few moments with my eyes open. Finally, I closed my eyes and fell into a deep, peaceful sleep—the kind that you want every night of the week—a perfect ending to another full day.

CHAPTER 6

Rude Awakening

"Bobby wake up! BOBBY WAKE UP! BOBBY WAKE UP!" I remember screaming to myself. This is a horrible dream. Why am I sitting in the dining room window? The dining room was next to my bedroom, and I was slumped over in the window sill. As I tried to pick up my head for the first time and shake out the grogginess, bright lights shone in my eyes from the right of me. I didn't know where they came from. I looked to my left and saw a haze, a cloud of smoke. A haze? A cloud of smoke? This seemed odd.

Lights flickered to my left through a big opening in my house wall and a startling, chilly breeze blew in. I tried to focus my eyes. At the same time, I smelled something foul: sulfur, tar, burning rubber, and burnt plastic. It was a horrible stench. A cold chill went through me, the kind that goes right to your bones. Again, I tried to focus my eyes and rub the crusty sleep out of them. BOBBY PLEASE WAKE UP! I was definitely in the dining room, and the wall between my dining room and bedroom was missing. It was gone. Completely gone. That didn't make sense. Where was the wall? How could a wall to a house be there one minute and gone the next? I saw the flickering lights again as my eyes came into focus. I stood there motionless and in utter disbelief. There in front of me was a full-size pickup truck. What? A pickup truck? I was now standing beside the front right tire. I shook my head, trying to shake the cobwebs out. *I must be dreaming. What's this truck doing in the middle of my dining room?* I remembered talking to Ava about the trick-or-treaters. Was this some horrible Halloween prank, I thought? *What's going on here? Is that a blue and white pickup truck in the middle of my house?*

I stood up the best I could. I was near the passenger door of the truck. The stench was stronger than ever, and a cloud of smoke surrounded me. Then I saw a man step out of the driver's side of the truck. He was a large man, scraggly in appearance, wearing a baseball cap. A gash sliced his forehead and something trickled down it. It was red but I couldn't completely focus to tell exactly what it was. I asked myself, *who is this man in the middle of my dining room?*

He saw me. "Is there somebody else in the house?" he asked.

Is there somebody else in the house? I thought. *Who is this strange man in the middle of my house?* His question echoed faintly in the back of my mind as I tried desperately to process thoughts coherently. *Is there somebody else in the house? What's this truck doing in the middle of my dining room? Is there somebody else in the house? Who's this strange man standing here asking questions? Where is my bed? What am I doing in the dining room? Is there somebody else in the house? What's this stench? What's this smoke? What is going on here? Is there somebody else in the house? SOMEBODY ELSE IN THE HOUSE? AVA! My wife! Where is my wife? Oh, please God, where is Ava?*

I freaked out and started running around the truck. I ran into my bathroom trying to turn on lights, thinking that if I could just get some light I could see more clearly what was going on. I flicked the switch in the bathroom, but for some reason, the lights didn't come on. That was odd. I ran out of the bathroom and back into my bedroom. I leaned up against the wall and searched with my right hand, probing, feeling for the switch. Finally, I found it, but it was no good—no lights. I ran into the kitchen—no lights. The hallway—none there either. The living room—the foyer—still none. I tried every single lamp. I even hit the switch for the TV—no dice. I couldn't get anything to work. There was no power anywhere.

I stumbled to the far side of the house to a second bathroom. I reached around the wall, flicked the switch and—*bingo*—lights came on. Relieved, I stepped into the bathroom. Something had been dripping on my legs. It was on my arms, too, but I didn't know what it was. I felt something crunch in my mouth, so I spit into the sink. I lifted up my head and looked in the mirror. I was groggy and my eyes had to try very hard to come into focus.

I stepped back in shock. I could barely see my face in the reflection in the mirror. There was a stream—a waterfall of red—flowing down my face. I could now tell that it was my own blood. I could now see it running down my chest and onto my arms, over my underwear and my legs, and onto the floor. I felt that crunching in my mouth again. Again I spit. Huge hunks of bloody glass plopped into the sink. I searched for a towel and found a white one. I turned on the faucet and put the towel under the water to dampen it. I wiped my face, thinking that if I cleaned up the blood, I'd have a better idea of how badly I was hurt. The towel made a scrunching sound as it scraped over pieces of glass that were imbedded in my cheek.

With the blood temporarily gone, I saw a huge hole in my cheek and stuck my tongue through it. Again, I spit a large chunk of bloody glass out of my mouth into the bowl. The blood had started to flow again from my face as I watched it splash into the sink. Wiping my face again, I threw the towel into the basin and turned to leave the bathroom. I slipped on the pool of blood now on my floor on the way out.

I walked through the hallway, past the other bedrooms, and into the main opening to the living room, not knowing where Ava was. I stood there for a second, trying to catch my breath from all the frenzy. As I looked into the room, the headlights from the truck blinded me and I couldn't get a clear view. I moved my head around to avoid the brightness of the beams. I then stepped around to the side and noticed that the front of the truck was in the back of my living room.

The man still stood there, leaning casually on the driver's door. He had a blank look on his face as if to say, "Where am I and who are you?" I glanced above the pickup and saw that the whole inside wall of my bedroom was completely gone. The only thing left of that wall was one two-by-four piece of wood dangling from the ceiling where the bedroom doorway used to be. Behind the pickup the whole back brick wall of the bedroom was completely gone. Street lights glowed outside. The lingering, thick haze gave these lights an eerie, surreal look.

I slowly crept toward the truck and looked around in the rubble. This rubble used to be my outside bedroom wall and my inside wall, the wall that separated my bedroom from my dining room. I saw broken bricks, splintered wood, pieces of plaster board. Shattered glass reflected the headlights. A mass of splintered plywood and broken sheetrock was all gathered up around the truck in a heap. My house was a complete mess.

My body began to tingle. I glanced underneath the truck. What in the world? There was a corner of our blue mattress. I looked closer and now I recognized the blue sheets. I leaned closer still and saw something moving underneath the truck—then it hit me! My eyes opened wide as it became apparent to me what had happened.

"God, *no!*" I shouted. "Ava's under the truck!"

I grabbed the truck and rocked it back and forth. I pushed. I lifted. Anything to move the truck off Ava. They say that sometimes in the heat of an emergency, adrenaline runs so high that it gives you the strength of ten men. I felt as if I had that, but still I could not move the truck at all.

I screamed for the man to help me move it. He stood there motionless and did nothing. "Why aren't you helping me? Why are you just standing there? Help me! Help me!" I screamed out for anyone to help me. "Somebody, please help me move this truck! My wife is under this truck!

Somebody, please help me save Ava! She's gotta be here. She's not anywhere else in the house. She's underneath this truck!"

My cries were in vain as if they fell upon deaf ears. I felt lonely and helpless. I stopped to catch my breath and looked at this man, puzzled about why he was still standing there and not helping me lift the truck. Then I heard banging on the front door. I ran to it and opened it up. In stepped an older black man. I had no idea who he was or why he was there. His eyes were filled with tears. They were hollow and transparent.

"Oh, my God," he cried. "I can't believe what just happened. I saw the whole thing happen."

I felt frozen and numb at that moment—partially feeling for him because I felt the emotion in his voice and from the look on his face—partially because it started to hit me—the impact of what he was saying, the desperation in his eyes. An icy chill ran through me like a sudden north wind that cuts you to the quick. I saw him put his hands down on his knees as his head slumped in disbelief.

Not knowing what to do, I ran past him out the door and down the street, two houses down. I banged on the front door of our neighbor's home screaming and yelling at the top of my lungs for him, his wife, his family— somebody to come and help me lift the truck up off of Ava.

Help! Help! Somebody please help me! My wife is under the truck! Help me, please! Somebody please help me! *Help! Help!*

I ran through the neighborhood in my underwear, a bloody mess, yelling and screaming for help. I turned around and ran back to my house. As I turned, I saw flashing lights in front of my home. A small crowd had gathered. I couldn't make out the faces of anyone.

Two paramedics grabbed me from behind when I ran back into the house—something any boy from Brooklyn reacts to by instinct—and I struggled to tear loose. They took me into the front bedroom and laid me on a couch. I was frantic and hysterical. I begged them to forget about me and to attend to Ava. "I'll be all right. I think Ava's under the truck. My wife is under the truck! See if she's okay. Don't worry about me!"

"You're going to be fine, sir. We have everything under control," one paramedic said. "We know where your wife is. Other paramedics are working with her. Just try to relax and calm down now for us, okay?" They kept assuring me that she was fine and everything was going to be all right.

"Call my wife's parents. They live close by. Let them know what's going on," I implored them.

"We'll call them soon. We need to take care of you," they reassured me. "We'll take care of Ava. It's going to be fine with both of you."

They talked about my injuries. Lacerations crisscrossed my face and burns covered different parts of my body. One injury startled me. "He has a broken left forearm," the shorter paramedic announced to the other.

"A broken arm?" I asked in disbelief. I had been trying to lift the truck and banging on a neighbor's door. "No way! I can't have a broken left forearm."

They assured me that I did. I then looked at my left arm and did a double take. It was swollen up to the size of a small watermelon. A deep indentation that looked like a tire mark and a tire burn with something black and dark was visible on it. My arm went limp every time I tried to move it.

By this time my arm was throbbing, my face felt as if it were on fire, and my heart was racing at two hundred miles an hour. The paramedics continued to assure me that Ava was okay.

Then, strangely, out of nowhere, a Bible verse popped into my head. It was a scripture that I remember learning in my early childhood—the Twenty-third Psalm: "Yea, though I walk through the valley of the shadow of death, I will fear no evil, for thou art with me."

This verse rang in my heart and my spirit, and I didn't know where it was coming from. Was God telling me something? Was I about to die? Was Ava about to die? What was going on? My mind was racing. I didn't know what was going on. I lay there crying, praying, and wondering.

All of a sudden, they loaded me on a stretcher, carried me out the front bedroom, wheeled me past the people outside, put me in the ambulance, and closed the doors. *Somebody please wake me up from this bad dream*, I pleaded in my mind.

As the ambulance drove away, I saw the house. I saw the lights flashing, people gathered in front of the house, and what looked like a huge opening in the side wall of the bedroom. I saw our house in the distance getting smaller and smaller. I wondered, *What happened to me? Where is Ava? Is she okay? Will everything be fine? And what in the world is going on here? Please help me find my Ava!*

CHAPTER 7

The Truth Hurts

On the way to the hospital I cried, prayed, screamed, and asked questions about Ava. "Where's Ava? I want to see Ava. Can you tell me what's happening to her?" I asked in desperation of the paramedic leaning over me in the back of the ambulance. I spit more glass out of my mouth and coughed out thick clots of blood. The paramedics didn't talk to me in any detail about Ava. They answered basic questions to calm me down, but didn't elaborate.

"We're attending to her. We know where she is," they said again. It was the same thing they told me in the house when I had asked earlier. I didn't like the feeling of being in limbo—of not knowing. It was starting to eat at me.

We arrived at Humana Clear Lake Hospital about ten minutes later, although it seemed like an eternity. My arm throbbed worse than ever. My face and body felt as if someone had set them on fire.

The doors opened and they wheeled me into the emergency room, then… they just left me there. They left me right there by myself. They must have known by this time that I was not in a life-or-death situation. I tried to calm down and began to come out of shock. I lay there in the hallway and saw the doctors and nurses talking about me in the distance. They would check on me every few minutes then walk away and confer some more. All the while I was thinking, *What the heck is going on? One minute I'm saying goodnight to my wife, the next thing I know there's a truck in my house. Then I'm lying in a hospital emergency room, and nobody's telling me what's going on.* I knew sooner or later that I was going to wake up from this terrible dream.

I propped myself up as best I could. A few minutes passed. What's happening with Ava? Why isn't she here yet? Why isn't anybody telling me what's happening with her? I sat for a few more minutes. Dazed. Confused. In silence.

Then I saw a man walking toward me. He was wearing a gray jacket, black slacks, and a gray shirt with a little white collar at the top. As he stepped up to my bedside, I looked at him.

"Are you Bobby Petrocelli?" he asked.

"Yes"—though reluctant to respond.

He introduced himself as the chaplain of the League City Police Department. He was silent for several seconds. He swallowed hard. I saw a lifetime in his eyes as he fought back tears. I thought to myself, *How does this man know who I am? Does he know me from my being a local teacher? Do I coach one of his children? Has he seen me at Lakewood Church? How does he know my name?*

"Listen," I said. "I don't know why I'm here. I don't know where my wife is. Nobody's telling me anything. Do you know what's happening? Will somebody please call my wife's family? Here's their phone number. They only live ten minutes away. Please call them. And where is Ava? Is Ava okay?"

There was an awkward silence. He again swallowed hard. I felt his uneasiness. His lip quivered and his nostrils flared with the strain.

"I'm sorry to tell you... that you wife did not make it."

Didn't make it? Didn't make it? I said to him, "Oh, I see... Ava's still at the house. She'll be here in a few minutes. She's on her way to the hospital. That's what you're telling me, right?"

"No, Bobby. You're wife did not make it."

I thought for a split second and then answered back, "She's still in the ambulance—on the way to the hospital. That *is* what you're telling me, isn't it? Please tell me that's what you're saying! She hasn't made it to the hospital yet! Right!

He hesitated for just a moment, then abruptly cut me off. He now spoke in a sharp, clear, no-nonsense tone. "No, Bobby. I'm sorry to tell you. Your wife did not make it. Your wife is dead."

I heard him that time. But I didn't say a word. Inside I was screaming out NO WAY! I was thinking that he has me confused with someone else. I just ate three bowls of pasta with her. We are going Thanksgiving shopping this weekend.

Numb—that's what I felt.

My arm throbbed. My face was on fire. But I felt numb.

How could Ava be dead? Not more than two hours earlier I had come home and eaten a bowl of pasta that she had made.

Dead?

We had watched *The Honeymooners* together and cuddled in the chair.

Dead?

We had talked about Nicholas' birthday, my family coming down for Thanksgiving, going early Christmas shopping on Saturday. How could she be dead? I couldn't believe this was true. This was some kind of sick, cruel dream. I was going to wake up soon. I just knew I was going to wake up.

I guess you could say I was in shock. I guess you could say I was in denial. But one thing I couldn't deny—I would never get Ava back. She had been stolen from me like a thief in the night, snatched from my arms in my very own house. We couldn't have been more secure, could we? Asleep in our home—locked up tight—a brick fortress around us. What could be safer than that? Yet somehow, it hadn't been enough.

The doctors didn't want to work on me until some family came to the hospital. I asked the chaplain to call the Dorsetts, and he did. Thinking about it now, I was upset with him for telling me that Ava was dead. I would rather the Dorsetts had told me. He told the Dorsetts on the phone that Ava had been fatally wounded and that I was in the hospital. There again, it would have been my preference for him to tell them in person rather than over the phone.

Mr. and Mrs. D. arrived shortly, and they were understandably hysterical. "Bobby, can you remember what happened? What happened, Bobby?" they asked with a frenzied desperation in their voice. They didn't know what had happened—whether we had been in a car accident or what. They were crying out that Ava was dead.

Bit by bit I was getting sketchy details of what had happened. I tried to piece it all together myself, but I didn't have enough information. I lay there for what seemed like an eternity. My body was beginning to tingle and, in other places, flashes of extreme pain shot through me. Blood seeped through the bandages over the wounds. I could feel the open gashes in my face, my leg, and my arm—the one where the bone had been severed in half. I don't know what hurt more: the physical pain of my injuries or the pain of feeling defenseless against what had happened to me in my sleep.

The Dorsetts called some of our friends: Tommy and Rachel Birchfield, Saleim, and other friends from Lakewood Church. Soon they were at the hospital. The district attorney who had come out to the scene of the accident happened to be the father of one my students. He recognized my name from the police scanner, so by morning, all of Santa Fe knew. Many friends, faculty, students, and staff from Santa Fe High School began pouring into the hospital that morning.

When Bill Dorsett, Mr. Dorsett's brother, called my family in New York to tell them about the tragedy, my sister Debbie answered.

"Hello, is this the home of Debbie Pulzone?" Bill Dorsett asked in a quivering voice.

"Yes, this is she," Debbie replied on the other end.

"There's been an accident involving Bobby and Ava... "

Debbie screamed and dropped the phone. "*Ahhhhhhhhhhhh!*"

My brother-in-law Nicky picked up the phone after Debbie became hysterical. Bill explained to Nicky what had happened and when he repeated the news to Debbie, they cried uncontrollably. Debbie told me later that this was one of the few times she had ever seen Nicky cry. This pain ran deep. Debbie then passed the word onto my mother who lived upstairs in the same house. The very next morning Debbie and my mother flew into Texas to be with me. That must have been some flight for them.

An hour later they stitched up my face. The hole in my right cheek was so big you could see my tongue through the side of it. They stitched up my right eye and removed glass fragments from my face and slivers from my mouth.

"Mr. Petrocelli, can you sit up at all, sir?" one nurse asked. I shifted my weight and tried to sit up, but couldn't pull myself fully upright. Using a scrub brush they tried to remove the tar and rubber that had been burned into my right arm, my leg, my back, and my left forearm.

"*Ahhhhhhhhhhhhhhhh!*" I screamed at the pain.

"I know this is painful, but we have to try and clean you as best as possible before we dress your injuries, Mr. Petrocelli," another nurse said.

They scrubbed and scrubbed and scrubbed, but finally realized that they couldn't get much debris out and would need surgery to remove it completely. My left forearm was indeed broken, the bone severed cleanly in half—not a pretty sight. They decided to put it in a temporary cast. "Bobby," the doctor told me, "we're going to have to do surgery and place a metal plate with screws in your arm to repair the bone and allow it to heal properly."

As I lay in bed, I tried to explain to Mr. and Mrs. Dorsett the sketchy details of what I knew about that evening. "All I remember was waking up slumped over in the dining room. Then I looked up and saw a full-size pickup in the living room and bedroom. Then a man stepped out of the side of the truck." Just as I mentioned this, the police walked by outside my open door—with the man. He was handcuffed and bandaged. He was being taken to jail after being treated.

Finally, I was taken upstairs to a private room. Tommy and Rachel were there with the Dorsetts. They prayed for me and tried to comfort me.

"Our most loving and merciful Heavenly Father, we come now into Your presence—hurt, confused, not knowing what to say, not knowing what to do, not knowing why You've allowed this terrible tragedy to happen. We do know, O God, that You promised to never leave us or forsake us. We need to know that right now, God. We feel left and forsaken. Bobby needs to know that You love him as a father loves his son."

I didn't look up, but I could hear someone starting to cry.

And then another, and another.

I couldn't contain my grief any longer, and the tears flowed freely from my eyes. I shivered as a cold chill ran over my body. Then I was embraced, carefully, yet lovingly, by the warm and welcome arms of my mother- and father-in-law and their family. It was the first comfort I had felt since the ordeal had begun.

Before I knew it, from the pain, emotion, and exhaustion, I dozed off to sleep. Several hours later, someone's watch alarm went off. "Ava, that's the alarm. It's time to get up," I said. I looked around the room and that's when it really hit me. I was still in the hospital.

Reality TV

It was now Friday, October 25, 1985. I spent the entire day in the hospital continually receiving calls from family and friends around the country, some of whom told me they were coming to Texas, others who sent condolences. Many people from Lakewood Church, Santa Fe High School, and our community continued to arrive to be by my side. A wave of sympathy and love flooded my hospital room. I was engulfed in their outpouring of love and emotion for both Ava and myself. It's what I needed to know—that I am truly loved by so many. Feeling their prayers and support lifted me up.

That night, while lying in my hospital bed watching the ten o'clock news, I saw the lead story. The reporter said, "Just when you thought your house was the safest place to be, then all of a sudden something like this happens..." They showed the video of my house and reported that a truck had come crashing through my bedroom wall. The news reported that Ava had been killed and I had been treated and released from the hospital. I screamed at the TV, "Oh, yeah. Then what am I doing here right now? Is this really happening? No way! I can't be in the hospital. Ava can't be dead and I'm alive. I'll wake up soon."

I left the hospital late morning on Saturday, October 26, 1985, knowing that I would have to return to have several surgeries performed, but, more importantly, thinking that I would have to bury Ava, my wife of only two and a half years. God please let this be a dream. OK, I am ready to wake up now. Let's go home and be back to normal. Was this a crazy dream? I can only hope.

Mr. and Mrs. D. drove me back to their house from the hospital. When I arrived at their house, hundreds of family and friends from all over the country were there to greet me. "Tears welled up in my eyes and a huge lump grew in my throat as I saw those who had come to be by my side. Many of them had dropped everything and had come within hours of hearing of the tragedy. I felt the compassion and unashamedly open rush of emotion from each of them. The magnetic force of God's love radiated from each one as they embraced me—a knowing that they were there for me—that they believed in me—that they would do everything in their power to help me through this day. I could not believe how many were at the house. Jay and his wife, the Leerish one, Jakey, Riv, Cheeks, Ava's best friend Toni (Swain) Fowler, her family and little sister Alli, who had cystic fibrosis and who was always so special to me.

I remember all of my friends' faces. They were so serious. Cheeks, who was always laughing and joking around, didn't crack a smile. Jakey, the other crazy one from school, was unusually somber and quiet.

Joe Liberatore (who left a hospital in Tulsa, where he had just had knee surgery) and Chris Harrison, teammates of mine from the ORU baseball team, had dropped everything and driven down from school. It meant the world to me that they had taken the time to be there—so much love, help, and support from so many. Even the Dorsett's neighbors who were out of town let us use their house to accommodate our guests. Some stayed for hours or days—others for weeks.

One of the most humbling experiences in my life was being bathed by my friends. I couldn't bathe myself due to my injuries. You know you have true friends when they're willing to carry you into the bathroom naked, lay you in a tub, and wash parts of your body you never thought they would bathe. To top it off, they argued over who would wash which parts. I consider these friends closer than brothers. It took them more than an hour to completely bathe me and wash my hair. Jay, the strongest of the fellas, lifted me up and held me while Riv washed my legs. Craig cleaned my arms. Cheeks rinsed off the soap. Joe Lib and Chris washed my back. Jakey shampooed and rinsed my hair. They all joked and rode each other about this, but it needed to be done, so they did it. I'll never forget the feeling of helplessness and the humiliation of not being able to bathe myself. This was eased because I knew how much these guys loved me as their brother. We had all been through so much together back at school at ORU. I could not have been in better hands. Riv joked that my bottom needed to be cleaned again and that Joe Lib would have to do it. Joe declined, saying, "That's Cheeks' area of expertise." "Jakey can fill in for me this time—I hate getting *behind* in my work," Cheeks grinned back at him.

We all had a good laugh. It reminded me of our old times together. It was a tremendously sad time for all, but despite the pain we all felt, we were able to laugh. This is how I would normally be with these guys—always joking and laughing. It felt good to laugh. It felt good to be with so many friends who loved Ava and me so dearly. The love never stopped flowing.

Day had now turned into evening. The fellas mentioned taking a ride. I overheard something about a "funeral home." I quickly dismissed that thought. Taking a drive and getting out would be great. It is Saturday—maybe Ava will keep our date. A movie, some spicy Mexican food, then a little shopping at the mall. Please God let me see Ava. Let me wake up? As we got into the car, the weather was miserable. Hurricane Juan, which moved into our area, was coming up from the Gulf to dump torrents of water on us. We drove through the darkness, the rain, and the fog. Driving, driving,

driving and joking around like everything was okay, normal, and fun. I remember finally pulling up in front of this building. "Where are we?" This doesn't look like the mall. Where is Casa Ole? Where's the movie theater? I remember they had mentioned something about seeing Ava, but it didn't register in my mind right away. Now Jay, Riv, Jakey, and Cheeks got really quiet. They opened the car door for me. I stepped out into the rain and realized I was in front of a building that read "Jack Rowe Funeral Home." "What are we doing here? Please don't tell me Ava is in here!"

Before I could do anything, my friends quickly escorted me into the building and walked with me as I hobbled through the foyer and up to a room with large, double doors. Out of the corner on my eyes I could see the Dorsetts with other family and friends. Jakey, Jay, Cheeks, and Riv opened the double doors, led me inside and then slowly, silently backed out, leaving me in the room by myself.

Why were they leaving me inside this room all by myself? I didn't know why. I hobbled around slowly, using crutches because the truck had run over my leg and burned tar and rubber into my thigh. I stood there just inside the door for a moment to take in the complete area I was standing in at that moment. It was a long, deep room.

I started toward the front and could see in the distance a lavender casket nestled amongst numerous flower arrangements. As I limped forward I began to realize there was a female in the casket. Closer I hobbled. Closer, closer, closer...

There was no mistake about it. It began to dawn on me. The woman in the casket was. . .Ava.

All the while that this had been taking place, I had still thought in the back of my mind that it *must* be a dream. It had to be. How could all of this have happened so quickly?

I ran to her, and screamed "Come on, Ava, this is not where we had discussed having our date. I want to go to the mall. I want to go to the movies! I thought we were going to Casa Ole? We have to go home now. This dream must end. This can't really be happening. It's time to wake up. I don't agree with you changing the location of our date. Please wake up!" I grabbed her and began lifting her out of the casket, placing her over my left shoulder.

My friends were peeking through the doors in the back of the room. When they saw me pulling Ava out of the casket, they rushed into the room and helped lay Ava back down. "I want to wake up. Bad dream. Halloween prank. Nightmare!!!" It now began to hit home. Like an anvil dropped on me from a second-story window, it hit me and nearly drove me into the pavement. Reality set in. It was now crystal clear—Ava was not sleeping. My wife, my college sweetheart, my Texas belle was DEAD!!!

Throughout Saturday night and all day Sunday, so many came to the funeral home in Clear Lake, Texas, to honor, revere, and respect Ava. Tears would change to laughter and back to tears again—emotionally like riding an upside-down roller coaster. It was as if I were watching this all take place in some other person's life—some TV show, movie, or crazy talk show. "Can this be happening?" I felt like an outsider looking in. Everything was eerily out of context—out of place. Loneliness. Fear. Hope. Love. Anxiety. Remorse. Depression—feelings were in constant fluctuation. My whole life, and the lives of literally thousands had changed drastically. I got to put up a front. I need to be strong and not let this get the best of me. I was a fighter— a staggered, beaten-up fighter. I had barely gotten up from the canvas before I was counted out. I had to answer the bell. I had to go the distance. Even so, the pain I had inside from losing Ava was more than I could bear. I couldn't hide it. I broke down and wept several times, sometimes alone, sometimes with others. There was no way I could keep it all bottled up inside. It hurt too much. It hurt way too much.

Monday morning, October 28, 1985,—the day of the funeral—was yet another rainy, dreary day. My friends again carried me and bathed me from head to toe. They dressed me in a suit, doing the best that they could, trying to work around my injuries. I rode in a limousine to Friendswood United Methodist Church, where Ava and I had been married, and which now would be the site of her funeral service. John and Dodie Osteen, from Lakewood Church (later to be pastored by John and Dodie's son, Joel), and Reverend Don Meador, from Friendswood United Methodist Church, officiated at the service. The pouring rain had not subsided for days. I was told it was from Hurricane Juan. I didn't buy it. It wasn't a hurricane. This was heaven crying and rejoicing. Crying because the earth had tragically lost such a precious life, but rejoicing because heaven gained another angel—an angel to look down on the rest of us. As the limo arrived at the church, I could see a foot of water covering the ground.

As I entered the church, I was enthralled. A church that normally seated about five hundred was packed to the hilt. Almost two thousand people were jammed into the building. The outpouring of love for Ava, me, and the Dorsett's was overwhelming. For the first time since the accident, as I walked into that packed sanctuary, I wept tears of joy. Over nine hundred and fifty of them were students from Santa Fe High School. Their love and affection poured forth. Words cannot express the feeling of being rushed, mobbed, and hugged by hundreds of students. The looks on their faces will live with me for the rest of my life. I realized my life had been spared for a special purpose.

In the service, the Osteen's gave the illustration of Moses during one of Israel's battles. As the story goes, as long as Moses' arms were raised up, the Israelites would win. When he got tired and dropped his arms, they began to lose. The Osteen's said that everyone as family and friends needed to be the ones to lift myself and the Dorsetts up in this time of need. We needed help to win this battle. We needed others to lift us up—to lift our hearts and spirits.

"Just as Moses needed his arms raised so that the Israelites would have victory, we ask You, O God, that You would help us to lift up Bobby's arms, the entire Dorsett family's arms, the Petrocelli family's arms—lift them up in victory, O Lord, that we might glorify You for Your strength to overcome—just as You have overcome death—to give us life eternal. Amen and Amen."

After the service, we drove twenty miles in the pouring rain to Forest Park Lawndale Cemetery in Houston. An enormous line of cars followed. It took over two hours to drive those twenty miles. The weather was miserable, but the support was immeasurable.

After orchestrating through the storm, we finally arrived at the cemetery. The pallbearers set the casket in place where Ava would be laid to rest. I watched this all from the limo, and when it came time, I stepped out of the solitude of the back seat into the wind- and rain-swept grass and mud, for a short service beside the grave. A small, green tent sheltered family members from the rain, and everyone tried to get under the tarp to keep dry. Several hundred crammed in tightly. The benediction concluded, "Ava Dorsett Petrocelli has surely stepped into His glory, where she will live with Jesus forever, our Lord and Savior." The minister asked us to leave. I wasn't ready to leave. We were married to each other for two years; it took two hours to drive twenty miles. I needed more than two minutes to say goodbye to her. I jumped on the casket sobbing my heart out. The only way my friends peeled me off was that they promised me we could return tomorrow.

As I returned to the limo, I stopped right before entering. I wanted one last look at the casket. This would be the last sight of physical evidence that I would have of Ava. As I turned to look, I froze in shock. Hundreds of students from Santa Fe High School were running towards me. Every one of them was soaked. Few had umbrellas. This was the second time it became clear to me why my life had been spared. Girls in high heels with mud up to their ankles—rain pouring down their faces—were getting some of the nappiest hairdos I would ever see. Boys in suits—soaked from head to toe—the rain didn't dampen their spirits. They were there for Coach Petrocelli. They love me that much. It truly touched my heart. My heart was full—full of love for the wife whom I had just laid to rest—and full of hope and tears for the young people whom I shall never forget who paid me the highest tribute on that rainy afternoon at Forest Park Lawndale Cemetery. It was the indelible support that, to me, will live in infamy.

The following is an excerpt from an anonymous letter that I received following the funeral that day:

"What impact has this tragedy had on your life and on mine— Well, I just recently attended her funeral service. The rains and winds of Hurricane Juan had worked our community over for hours prior to Ava's funeral, and yet those forces could not stem the flow of people into the United Methodist Church. The church's parking lot was full and the paths to the church were under water, but that did not stop them either. They came with coats, with umbrellas, without coats, without umbrellas. They came in groups, and they came alone. Older people, younger people, teenagers, housewives, businessmen, church members, non-church members, Christians, and non-Christians—they came and they came. The church was filled, the hallways were filled, but most of all—their lives were filled by the spirit and the love for Bobby and Ava that I saw demonstrated that day. Their hair was wet and bedeviled by Hurricane Juan, their shoes oozed water, their clothing was mistreated and damp, but they were there.

I wish all of you reading this could have been there in that church also. To begin with, it was the first church service of any kind where I had to stand in line just to get in! And then, once inside, the task of moving around was even harder. There was a long line of people, mostly young people, filing steadily by the casket. It seemed an unending line.

As the service progressed and passages of scripture were read and songs were sung, the crowds in the foyer, who stood eight people deep, were solemn and reverent. Their hair was doused, their feet were soaked, their spirits were dampened, but they stood fast, and they stood quietly. They were as diverse a group as you could imagine, and yet they had a common bond—love. Yes, they loved Ava and they love Bobby, and the love that was throughout that solemn service was transferred. This love was so easy to see and even easier to feel. I am glad I was there to share that love. I am glad I knew Ava. So be like Bobby and be like Ava—be good servants and increase your gifts tenfold so that your life will be a light to all those in darkness.

Do not allow your tragedy to catch you in the dark without ever letting your light shine and shine and shine."

CHAPTER

Reality TV Too

After the burial we returned to the Dorsett's house. Our families and our closest friends were there to talk and have something to eat. Friends from all over the area had dropped off food for us. I was continually amazed by the outpouring of love and caring from so many people after the tragedy. When things like this happen, it seems to bring out the best in people with everyone forgetting about themselves and trying to be helpful in any way possible. With all the stories and news of everything bad happening in the world, this was something good. It strengthened my faith.

About a week afterwards, most of my family and friends returned home—back to their different states and back to their own lives. I was grateful that they had come to support me in my time of pain, but I knew that each one of them would eventually have to leave, and that I would be facing this fight without them. When someone experiences loss, there is such an outpouring of love. But then everyone eventually returns to their normalcy. What was my normalcy going to be now? Would anything ever seem normal to me? Those who experience loss now have to find what normalcy is without their loved one. I share with others that it's the minutes, hours, days, weeks, months, and even at least a year after the loss, that you search for what is normal. I think at the funeral, those who experience the loss should pass out cards. The cards should have future times when you need that loved one to contact you. "Please call me one week from today"; "call me in three days"; "please take me out to dinner two weeks from now"; and so on. It's when their life is back to normal and you are still in the middle of the pain that you need support.

Over the next few days after Ava's burial, infection started to set into my body. I tried for a few days to delay going back into the hospital, but my orthopedic surgeon ordered me to go in immediately to have the surgeries performed before further problems could develop.

For two days prior to the surgeries, IVs with fluids and antibiotics fought the infections and flushed out the sickness that was invading my body. Jakey was with me. My mother and my sister Debbie were there. The Dorsetts also came to be with me.

Students from Santa Fe High School continually stopped by. From morning until night, students poured into the hospital in a constant stream. They took over the floor, my room, the hospital wing, the elevators, the staircases, the lobby, and even the hospital parking lot. Everyone was amazed at their response and the magnitude of their outpouring of love for me. They brought every type of food, incredibly beautiful flower arrangements of every kind, a zoo full of stuffed animals, every variety of candy known to mankind, and so many supportive and creative get well cards that there was no way I wasn't going to get well. Some were special cards—rolled paper cards that reached more than a hundred feet long. It included signatures, sayings, greetings, and well wishes from every single student at Santa Fe High School. They had rolled out the sheets in the cafeteria at school where students, faculty, and staff had signed them. These are still very special gifts that I have saved over the years to remind me of their genuine love and support for their Coach Petro. Each day that they came confirmed to me why my life was spared: to try and make a difference in the lives of young people.

The nurses on the fourth floor were incredible, allowing nonstop visitors, morning 'til night. They never made me abide by the posted visitors hours which were supposed to end at ten o'clock each night. Though I had a semi-private room, no other patients were placed in there with me. The nurses did all they could to accommodate me. They were truly special. They realized that I was hurting both physically and emotionally. I not only had physical injuries to be dealt with, but the loss of Ava was overwhelming, and I needed all the love and support possible. The practice of good bedside manner is essential in the medical world. I know how much it helped me. Everyone knew their role to help with the recovery process. Again, actions spoke louder than words. I felt genuine concern and compassion from the nurses on my wing. It transcended what we would normally think of as "hospital care." It was a special kind of nurturing and loving care that I felt from them constantly.

The next days were very, very difficult. I had known the surgeries would be painful, but I had no idea how painful. I guess it's better that I didn't know. Some things you're better off not knowing about. This was one of those things. When the truck had crashed through the brick wall that tragic night, the spinning tires literally burned rubber from the truck tires into various places on my body. Just like rubber burned into the highway, the same skid marks were embedded into my skin. Several times that week, several times each and every day, the physical therapist took me to the rehab room. He placed me in a hot whirlpool bath with the purpose of softening and loosening up the skin in those affected areas on my body so that he could use tweezers to try and pluck the dead skin, the tar, and the burned-in rubber off of my body. You know how painful a splinter in your hand is? Imagine a rubber splinter that has been burned into or even melted into your hand— that's what had happened to me, except both tar *and* rubber had been burned into my arm, my leg, my back, and my abdomen. These pieces were much larger than a little splinter. The physical therapist kept plucking and plucking—plucking and plucking. Deeper and deeper he dug—constantly digging, digging, and digging. This was nothing short of absolutely excruciating pain. It was torture. "Please John, isn't there any other way?" "Bobby, if there were any other way I could remove the rubber and the tar, I would. You've got to believe me. The problem is, it's embedded and literally melted into your skin," the physical therapist told me for the fourth time that week. He could see my agony.

Still, I soaked and soaked and soaked in the whirlpool. Then once my skin was soft, he would go to work on me. "*Ahhhhhhhhhhhhhh,*" I would yell in pain. He would stop only momentarily—just long enough for me to stop screaming—then would continue digging and plucking until I couldn't take it anymore and I screamed in agony again. He would stop, I would fight the pain, scream, and then the whole cycle would begin again. I hated it. It was nauseating. Overwhelming. Throbbing. My heart goes out more than ever to burn victims. This was the most physical discomfort I would experience. Several times I almost passed out. I got dizzy from the combination of pain and fatigue from fighting the pain. I dreaded every minute. I would hate to see another person have to go through what I had to go through. After four days of this treatment, the PT finally determined that my case was too severe. He confirmed the doctor's diagnosis: The rubber had been seared into not only my skin, but seared into the very muscles as well. On my fourth day in the hospital, Dr. Boone repaired my left forearm with a bone graft from my hip. A steel plate was set in there also. In addition, surgeons removed the rubber and tar. Lucky me. The removal of the rubber left my body with a gaping hole in my upper right arm and right quadriceps until the skin graft could be performed.

As I lay in the recovery room, I felt my arm throbbing again. It was a familiar feeling. The tar and rubber removal process had been especially difficult, the doctor told me, because it had burned so deeply into my muscle. I now had to lie on my back for an entire week to recover, and strengthen myself for the next set of surgeries. Dr. Chin, the plastic surgeon, placed pig skin over the quadriceps opening. Next up was a skin graft.

Seven long days I was laid up in that hospital room. Everyone was absolutely wonderful to me, but I had a lot of time just to lie there and think. So for the next several days, that's exactly what I did. I would lay there and think. I had so much to think about.

What am I going to do with my life now? I asked myself. *What's the next step?* Do I still have a purpose? A lot was going around in my head. The Dorsetts had made it clear that I was welcome to stay with them for as long as I needed. I could even stay until the following summer if need be. I didn't know if I should go back to teaching and coaching, move somewhere else, or stay around the area. I wasn't sure. I had come to Texas primarily to be with Ava. Did I really have a reason to stay here now? She had been my partner—my partner for life. What kind of life was I going to have now? Was I going to be alone for the rest of my life? Was that my destiny? To be alone? I'm a firm believer that everything happens for a reason—somehow, there must be a reason?

"There must be a reason. There must be a reason. There must be a reason?" I said. I searched and searched, but found no reason—none anywhere. Like a blind man searching for a light switch in a darkened cave—that's how I felt. I needed a bright ray of hope, but first I needed to regain my sight. A cloud loomed over my head. I prayed that God would bring sunshine back to my heart. The joy of my life had been taken away, snatched from my very arms. My heart felt as if a lead weight had been placed in it and I couldn't move it by myself. I needed help from outside sources—ones who would never leave me nor forsake me—who would stay with me forever.

Over the next week, Dr. Chin would have to remove skin from my inner right thigh and graft it to the opening on my right thigh and right upper arm. I asked him to give me a saddle block—a long needle in my spine to numb the lower part of my body. I didn't want to be totally knocked out. I was emotionally drained after the first set of surgeries and had a fear of being put out again. I didn't enjoy the first experience of being under. The emotional state I was in compounded my situation. He was willing to accommodate me—that's what made even my medical team special. God always knows what *we need* to get through. He doesn't send the pain, but sends the help to make it more tolerable.

I watched as Dr. Chin used a tool resembling a cheese slicer to remove the skin from the inner part of my right thigh. Since I would have to be in bed for an entire week of recovery, Dr. Chin did not want the skin to be taken from my backside. It would have been more difficult to the find a comfortable lying position. For the next entire week I was confined to bed, lying on my back. A whole week seemed like an eternity—not an hour, or just an afternoon, but an entire week. It was like I was voluntarily paralyzed in that position. I couldn't shift around to a more comfortable position. I couldn't even roll to my side or stomach, because of the possibility of reopening the leg wound. It was like being a confined prisoner in bed. The lack of movement began to really drive me crazy. I was an athlete and used to moving freely and fluidly.

I had been in the Humana Clear Lake Hospital for nearly three weeks, and now it was the day before Thanksgiving and I was finally getting out of the hospital. Ah, Thanksgiving, it's usually my favorite holiday, a time for family to get together and be thankful for blessings. I remembered that my family was supposed to be coming down to visit Ava and me and spend the holiday at our new home. To top it off, my birthday was on Thanksgiving Day. Twenty-five-years-old but I feel like I am one hundred and twenty-five. Thanksgiving is a time to be grateful, and a lot of people tried their best to tell me that I still had things to be thankful for. Did I? Did I really? It's easy to be an onlooker and say that. But they hadn't been through what I'd been through. It's tough to be thankful and content in all situations.

Does anybody really think they can feel what I've been feeling? I had done nothing to deserve this, yet my life was changed forever. I now had to start from Ground Zero. Could I piece my life back together? My wife had been stolen from me. The future we had was gone. I had barely escaped with my own life. Was I supposed to put on a happy face and be grateful? It was hard to remember to be thankful. However, I was thankful that my injuries were not worse. I could've easily been in a worse condition but I was thankful for all the love that had surrounded me—and thankful, I guess, that I was still alive.

CHAPTER

10 Seconds

In the car on the way to their home in Friendswood, a trillion thoughts raced through my mind, all at the same time. My mind was channel surfing. I was on my way back to the Dorsett's house. Mr. and Mrs. D. had told me again that I was welcome to live with them for as long as I needed. I thought that was very generous of them, especially the fact that I would continually remind them of Ava.

During my three weeks in the hospital I had mostly watched television, listened to music, and most of all, thought. How much thinking can one person do? Please, enough already. I had thought a lot about this day—the day I would finally leave the hospital. I thought about what I would do when I stepped into their home to live with them while I recuperated. Remembering the first visit I had while dating Ava, my senior year of college, Christmas break—I was nervous then and petrified now. Would they also be reminded of that time? Would all of us be reminded of our visits? I had thought about what I would say to Mr. D. when I first walked through the door. What could I say to them that wouldn't sound rehearsed? What could I say to Randa, Ava's younger sister, so as not to make it obvious that she would see me, but never her sister again? I didn't know the answer to any of these questions. I didn't have a premeditated greeting for any of them. I just wanted to say what I felt. And what I felt was a lot of pain. They must be feeling the same pain? I had lost my wife and that wife was their daughter. What can you say to that?

Mrs. D. (Momala as she was affectionately called) was the one who picked me up from the hospital. When I arrived at their house, Mr. D. was out running an errand and Randa was at school. Momala was warm towards me and made me feel welcomed as she began working on some chores in the kitchen. I had thought about doing something in particular, a lot. It was something that I planned but didn't discuss with anyone. Since Mr. D. and Randa were gone, it would be easier for me to get away. This thing that I wanted to do was starting to eat at me really bad. So I did it. I was still on crutches, but I did it. I snuck into Mr. and Mrs. D.'s bedroom and got the keys to my 1983 maroon Toyota Celica GT. Mrs. D. figured out that I was going—she had that sixth sense. She knew. She was quite upset that I was going to go—but I had to. "Bobby you are in no condition to drive." I had to drive over to my house to see the entire scene of the tragedy. I had to go. There were no two ways about it. I absolutely had to see it for myself. I needed to somehow figure out how all this could have happened. It was too crazy and far fetched. This was too much of a freak accident—though the word "accident" doesn't begin to describe it. I had to see how in the world a full-size pickup truck had ended up in the middle of my house. "Please Momala I need to go. I'll be fine. I have to go myself." She was concerned, but I was convincing. I absolutely had to see for myself what had happened, even though it might be extremely painful to relive.

The drive from Friendswood to League City, about seven miles, was especially painful. This was the exact route that Ava and I had driven countless times when returning from her parents' home. Route 518—this road was better known as FM 518. They say that women remember everything. I know a guy whose memory is pretty good, too. A flood of thoughts rushed through my mind—like a roller coaster of emotions—up and down, up and down—remembering so many times that Ava and I would take this route. The ten-minute drive took thirty as I finally arrived in League City—a place that I had called home for only two months. Why did we move here? Did we have to rent that specific house? If we didn't, Ava should still be alive. The moment of truth was here. This was the first time I had returned to the house since the night of the tragedy. I was hoping to find some answers to the questions that were eating me up inside. What will I see there? Do I even want to see it?

I slowly pulled into the entrance of our housing development. On the right side was the grassy field, Petro's Greens. I saw our house at the far end of it in the distance. It was very weird looking at our house in this manner— kind of like a stranger looking on from the outside—as if I had heard about some tragedy happening to other people and I wanted to see for myself. It was a very odd feeling. Was this actually the place I used to call my house? Did I really live here? Did this really happen? It was all too surreal.

I slowed down and stopped short to get a full view. Tire tracks sliced across the grass field. They were straight and crisp, almost as if someone had drawn them with a straight-edge. They traveled on a beeline straight to the side wall of our house taking out the brick wall of our bedroom. The only problem now was the wall was completely gone, covered now by plastic and wood to keep out the rain. The plastic had since ripped and was blowing in the wind. It was a scary sight—looking at the house from the distance like this. It was off by itself at the end of this piece of land—like a set from a movie.

Let me explain how our housing development was arranged. Our neighborhood complex sat off of the road named Farm to Market Road 518, the main street in League City. Our entrance to the development was about a half mile from Interstate 45. The road was called North Landing Boulevard. We lived at 501 North Landing Boulevard. Two lanes entered the development

and another two lanes exited it. A divided median with trees and shrubs separated the four lanes. Our house was the first one on the right entering the
grounds about a quarter of a mile in, at the end of the long, grass-covered
field. This field was on the right as you turned in the development, and
another grassy field mirrored it on the left. This property was eventually going
to be used for shopping centers. I looked at the skid marks on both sides of
the median—the tracks going across the median, up over the curb, through
the field, and directly to the house. This was insane. It was too perfect. For
someone to follow the straight path I was now looking at was unimaginable.

According to the police report, at approximately 12:35 a.m. on Friday,
October 25, eyewitness Jay Lane Ledbetter had been leaving the development. Jay reported that he had just dropped off a fellow worker when he saw
a light blue and white Ford F150 4x4 pickup truck enter the inbound lanes.
The thirty-seven-year-old male truck driver swerved and fish-tailed on North
Landing Boulevard. Jay stated, "The truck gunned it—and really pushed
it—coming in. I said to myself, 'Hey, if he doesn't slow down, something is
going to happen.'"

A black Camaro pulled into the complex behind the pickup truck. The
man driving the black Camaro was the same man who later banged on the
front door of my house telling me that he saw the whole thing happen. Jay
slowed down and watched. The truck, out of control, hit the concrete
dividing median, went over the median, and into the two exiting lanes. It was
now driving on the wrong side of the road for about thirty feet. Then,
without warning, it crossed back over the median again, across the two
incoming lanes. The full-size pickup then hit the curb and rode over it.

The truck sped across the grassy field, traveling 313 feet, which is more
than the length of a football field. It proceeded on a direct path toward the
brick wall on the side of the house. Judging by the distance, it was estimated
that the truck was traveling approximately sixty-five to seventy miles per
hour when it crashed through the wall.

The truck crashed directly through our outside brick bedroom wall. The
tire marks were so perfectly straight that it looked as if someone had
purposefully driven into that area of the house. I said it before, but it was
really weird—oh, how really eerie and weird. It was as if the back brick

bedroom wall had been a target—like there was a spot marked for the truck to aim for and hit.

I sat there and looked again at the skid marks, the tire marks, and the massive, gaping hole in the house where the wall used to be. It is frighteningly unimaginable. When a car is traveling 60 mph, it is proceeding at about 88 feet per second. For a car to be traveling 70 mph, it had to be moving more than 100 feet per second. That means, considering the length of the field and the speed that it was traveling, it took him about three seconds to come across the grass and crash through our brick wall.

As the truck crashed through the wall, it went airborne for an instant as a result of hitting the foundation slab of concrete under our home. I was sleeping about four to five feet from the wall. The truck landed on top of me and ran over me completely. The tires, still spinning, burned hot rubber into my body on my arm, leg, back and abdomen; then it threw me up on top of the hood. It then carried me through the bedroom, past the inside bedroom wall, and threw me all the way across the room and into the dining-room window at the back of the house at which point my face shattered the window and I came to rest in a slumped position in the window. That's where I woke up, in a stupor, now sitting in the dining-room window.

Unbeknownst to me, while I was riding on the hood of the truck, Ava was underneath it being rolled up in the sheets and the mattress. As the truck continued through the house, Ava was being dragged along.

The truck plowed through our bedroom, through the wall between the bedroom and dining room, crashed through the dining-room table, and into the chairs that were in the back part of our living room. The front of the truck was now resting in our living room after traveling about twenty-five feet through the house. The cab was in the dining room. The tail end of the truck was in the back of our bedroom. Buried underneath the truck was Ava.

The paramedics later told us that when the truck landed on her, it most likely knocked the air out of her body. Simultaneously, the sheets and the mattress wrapped around her face and body so tightly that she never got another breath of air. She died of asphyxia due to suffocation. She suffocated to death in the sheets of our bed. This thought of how she died horrified me. The ironic thing is that she had no broken bones and hardly a mark on her body. But it had taken them thirty minutes to dig her out from underneath the rubble, and when they finally got to her, she was dead.

So there I was. I sat silently numb in my car at the entrance of our housing development, thinking about all this, running it over and over in my mind—replaying the whole scenario in my mind. I was visualizing everything—rewinding it, playing it, rewinding it, playing it, rewinding it, playing it—over and over in the imaginary VCR in my mind. The scene played, rewound, played, rewound, and played. Dozens and dozens of times the scene raced through my mind. I looked again and again at the skid marks and the seemingly perfectly grooved tire lines in the grass on the way toward the house. I visualized the truck crashing through the house, running over me and Ava, going through the inner bedroom wall, and ending up in the back part of our living room.

Two things started to dawn on me more than ever. First of all, this could have been prevented. This whole thing could have easily been prevented. Why? The man driving the three-quarter-ton pickup truck had a blood alcohol content of almost .20. It was actually .19. At this time in 1985, in Texas and in most states, to be considered legally drunk a person's blood alcohol level had to register a .10. (Presently, most states are moving to make .08 the legal level for intoxication.) So, therefore, he was considered double legally drunk.

I was told on that particular day, October 24, the driver of the pickup had had problems at his job and had gone to three different bars, drinking for most of the day. Then, after his final stop in a bar in Clear Lake, he had left, thinking that he could drive home. That's when he drove into my neighborhood, lost control of his vehicle, crashed through our home, killed Ava, severely injured me, and changed lives—including his own—forever.

I lost a wife. The Dorsetts lost a daughter. Randa lost a sister. Friends lost a friend. Aunts and uncles lost a niece. Even the drunk driver lost his family since his wife and children eventually left him. And on top of this—my hospital bills totaled around $25,000. This was in 1985. By the standards of 2005, my medical bills would have been over $100,000. Tragedies are costly in every sense of the word. Any form of abuse will always catch up. Irresponsibility affects us all. It steals, kills and destroys. It takes and takes and takes—and it doesn't give back!

The second thing that dawned on me, as I calculated the whole situation, was that this tragedy could not have taken more than ten seconds—*three seconds to travel the grass field—three or four seconds from when he first turned into the development and two to three seconds when he hit the wall, ran over me and Ava, crashed through the next wall and came to rest in our living/dining rooms. Put it all together—approximately ten seconds—ten seconds or less!* That's all it had taken for a foolish, irresponsible decision to be made. Ten seconds for a man to drive into our complex, lose control, hit the curb, cross the field, come through the wall, kill my wife, hurt me, and ruin our lives. Ten seconds! Ten seconds! All of our hopes and dreams for a happy marriage and future together were taken from us in an instant—by a man who decided to drink and drive. Ten seconds—that's all it takes to change a life—not a week, not a day, not an hour—not even a minute. But just ten seconds.

I sat there quietly for several minutes thinking about this as tears rolled down my face. It was a hard fact to swallow—that such a short time could have such a long impact.

I don't remember anything of the drive back to the Dorsetts. I can't even remember how long it took me. All I could think about was *that* ten seconds. My mind was too numb to think of anything else.

Ten seconds can change a life forever. Ten seconds can and will change your life forever!

CHAPTER 11

Can I Ever Live Again?

The Dorsetts' house felt completely different to me now. This was to be my new home, at least temporarily, so I saw things with new eyes. I saw more detail. I paid attention to more of the little things around the house—the pictures on the refrigerator, the pattern on the wallpaper, the style of the furniture in the living room. It's like the difference between driving to someone's house one time and being a passenger the next time that you go to the same house. You pay more attention when you are the driver. The reality of being there was settling in. I had been there countless times visiting with Ava, but it was odd actually living there.

On the day before Thanksgiving, all kinds of thoughts were going through my head. Will I ever live again? Will I ever enjoy life again? Will I ever find happiness again? Will I ever experience joy? Can I enjoy going to the beach knowing what I look like now, after being disfigured? Will I have to go to movies by myself? Can I ever look at a sunset and not think of watching it with Ava? How will my time with her parents be? Can I enjoy the holidays at all?

I was lonely and anguished. I was stuck in a situation that I hadn't caused. I didn't deserve this. Why was this happening to me?

I thought about the kids at school. Would I go back to teaching and coaching at Santa Fe? What would my future hold? Should I stay in the League City area? Should I go back to New York? What was the right thing to do?

One bright ray of hope that day was Saleim, my close friend.

"Petro!" his voice said on the other end of the phone.

"Saleim, what are you up to, buddy?" I asked. Hearing his voice was a comfort in itself.

"Let's go see *Rocky 4* tonight."

"It sounds good, boss. What time do you want to go?" I asked excitedly.

Saleim was excited, too. I could tell by the tone of his voice. I'm a big Rocky fan and I was eager to see the newest film of the series. It was a good diversion for me, also, because I enjoyed being with Saleim, and I needed to be able to temporarily escape from all the pain. It gave some sense of normalcy. He had been my friend before the tragedy and, of course, our friendship continued. I felt, even for the moment a sense of security—being with a great friend and watching a movie that gave me hope. Love is important, and faith is necessary. But hope is essential.

After the movie, we went to get something to eat. Saleim was my best buddy while living in the Houston area. He was athletic, a solid guy, and fun to be with. He reminded me of a lot of my buddies from college. He could have been one of "the boys." Saleim worked at Houston Baptist University and, while I had been in the hospital, he had driven more than a hundred miles every night to hang out with me. He would leave straight from work and oftentimes would stay until past midnight, then drive back. Many times

The story of my triumph over tragedy is one based on the foundations laid during my childhood, which held strong to bring me to where I am today. (Inset) My sister Debbie and I, during one of the few moments she wasn't getting me into trouble.

The Petrocelli family in Brooklyn, Debbie, Mom, Dad, Chrissy, and me.

My sisters and I are still close to this day. (See the resemblance to Travolta?)

Dad, Mom, Debbie and I, with Grandma and Grandpa Petrocelli

The summers in the Catskills were great times with Nanny, Beepa and family. (Scandinavians love to travel to the mountains.) Being Italian and Swedish, I'm a true Swedish Meatball.

My cousins Mary Jo, Vinny, and I at our high school graduation. (True Italians all have a cousin Vinny.)

The Petrocelli family at my Uncle Davey and Aunt Dotty's 50th wedding anniversary. (We Italians love to gather and eat.)

One of my favorite pictures of all times. Uncle Rico, Dad, and I in Fenway Park in Boston. It was always a great thrill to go to major league games at Fenway and Yankee Stadium to watch Uncle Rico play. (Inset) I had my own dreams of being a major leaguer one day.

Oral Roberts University in Tulsa, Oklahoma, where more friendships and foundations were established. I fought for a spot on the Top 20 ranked Titans, but my baseball-playing days ended here with graduation.

The "fellas"—Cheeks, me, Riv, Jay, and Jake. (Riv thought he was the Godfather.)

Ava Lynn Dorsett Petrocelli, my Texas Belle.

The Dorsett's and I: Randa, me, Ava, Mr. and Mrs. D. (Linda and Randall).

I will never forget the students at Santa Fe High School for their love and support.

*This is the freshman football team and girls varsity track team
I was coaching during the school year of 1985 and 1986.*

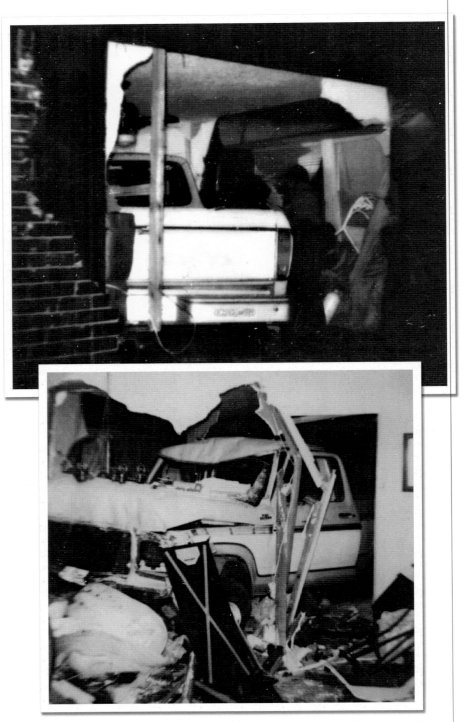

The blue and white pickup truck, driven by a man twice legally drunk, crashed through our bedroom wall traveling 70 mph as we slept.

All that remained of the wall between our bedroom and dining room was shattered sheetrock and a two-by-four with the smoke alarm. The window on the far left (bottom photo) was where I awoke that tragic night.

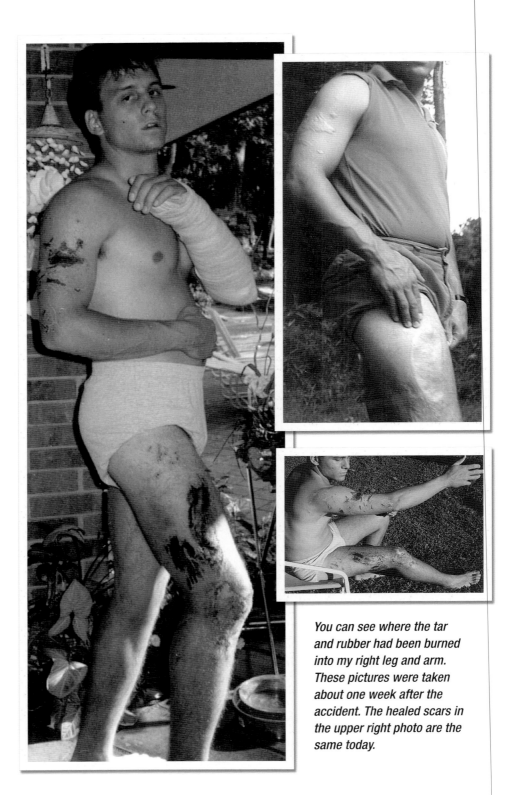

You can see where the tar and rubber had been burned into my right leg and arm. These pictures were taken about one week after the accident. The healed scars in the upper right photo are the same today.

Could I ever love again? Suzy is my most precious gift. Suzy and I on our wedding day. Sixteen years later and still going strong. Doing our favorite thing, taking a cruise!

Alec and I with one of my
inspirations and heroes—Rocky!

Daddy's champs—Alec and Aron
Petrocelli! And let's not forget
Rocket, our wild rat terrier. They
all look just like their Daddy!

Doing what I love doing the best—traveling and spending time with the family.

Bobby signing an autograph after a life-changing message.

Bobby giving an inspirational message.

Students discussing Bobby's latest book.

Bobby sharing his inspiring story with people of all ages.

TV personality Geraldo Riviera and I after a taping of his show.

Little did I know the positive impact I would have on so many precious lives. Students securing copies of my inspirational books.

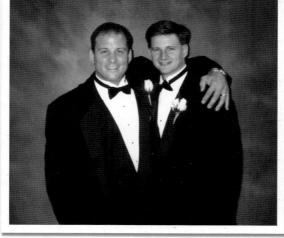

Brad Hurdle and I—Brad came to hear me speak after also losing his wife to a drunk driver. A few years later, after developing a friendship, he asked me to be a groomsman in his wedding.

Bobby captivating his audience. Wow!

Lives changed. Incredible!

Impacting a life forever. Priceless.

he would take a nap in a hospital chair as he stayed to early morning and go directly to work. That's a dedicated friend. Love, faith, and hope are actions. It was an escape from my hospital routine. I would look forward to him coming every day. I didn't have to dwell on why I was in the hospital in the first place—and I was not all alone.

I woke up early on Thanksgiving Day. Mr. and Mrs. D., Randa, and I were driving up to Palestine in East Texas to spend the holiday with Grandma Dorsett. Sitting in the back seat with Randa for the three-hour drive became awkward, and I tried to joke around and make the trip seem a little shorter.

But everyone in the car was thinking the same thing: Thanksgiving is supposed to be a time to be happy and thankful. How could we hide the fact that we hurt so much inside? I knew it was painful for the Dorsetts to drive all the way there with me—happy in one sense to have a son-in-law—but grieving over losing their oldest daughter.

Throughout the journey I thought of Ava. I desperately wanted Ava to share Thanksgiving and my birthday with me. My family would have been with Ava and I in our new home. None of us could muster up the courage to look each other in the eye for too long. We each cried out in our own way, looking for some reason, some unknown reason that this had taken place. The answers were not coming. We hoped someday they would.

Grandma Dorsett had cooked up a tremendous spread of food: turkey, stuffing, potatoes, greens, cranberries, cornbread—the works. We sat around the table anticipating the home-cooked feast. When she emerged from the kitchen carrying the turkey, however, her eyes fell on the empty chair where Ava would have sat, and we all momentarily stared silently at it. Her happiness quickly dissipated. She mustered up a false smile, but it was as empty as the chair.

We tried to enjoy the food, but the chair sat empty, a reminder of Ava. In past years by this time we would have been talking and laughing at stories that Grandma told about Mr. D. and his childhood. There were no stories this year. There was very little talking. No one knew what to say. Most questions were answered with a nod of the head or a quick glance in that person's direction. Most of the time, none of us made eye contact. We didn't want to see the pain and sorrow that filled each of our hearts—the pain that was mirrored in our eyes and that shook our very souls.

"So, Randall, how's business going?" Grandma asked. Mr. D. just nodded without looking up or speaking a word. The rest of us stared at our plates and ate. We mostly looked at each other with our peripheral vision—never looking directly at each other at all.

The silence and awkwardness was so staggering that I got up from the table several times and went into the bedroom—and cried. I couldn't get over the fact that she wasn't there. It's November 28th. How could I have a happy birthday? I was a quarter of a century old and in immense pain. I truly tried to be thankful for something—the kids at Santa Fe!

After the holiday break is when I decided that I would return to teaching at Santa Fe High School, so I notified the school of my decision. I had mixed feelings about the decision because I didn't know how I would react to being with the kids again. Could I face the kids? Could I look at them? Could I enjoy teaching as I had before? I knew this was probably the best thing to do—to get back into spending time with the kids and to get my mind off the tragedy. I had to try and move forward with my life. Physically, I had recovered well enough to resume my teaching duties. Emotionally, I knew I could count on the kids. I was so touched that they had supported me throughout the whole time—at the funeral in the pouring rain, at the cemetery in the mud, and at the hospital while I was recovering. What could I say to them? Would I break down and cry? How would my first day go?

The drive to school on December 2, my first day back since the tragedy, was long. Each minute seemed like an eternity. The reason was that this was new to me—new from the fact that I never had worked at Santa Fe High School without Ava physically in my life. When I pulled into the parking lot, I sat in the car for a few moments before opening the door to get out. I still had my doubts.

A few students saw me as I got out of the car. "Coach Petro's back. Coach Petro's back," I heard them say in the distance. For an instant I thought that I should act as if I hadn't heard them, but instead I waved and gave them the thumbs-up sign. They hesitated, staring at me, not knowing how to respond. They smiled, gave me thumbs-up and excitedly jumped up and down. Their joyful responses lifted my spirits.

I felt as if everyone's eyes were glued on me as I walked into the building, and they probably were. I don't know if they were in disbelief or shocked to see me walking the halls again. Chills and goose bumps ran through me from the feeling of being inside the school again—as if I were a stranger everyone knew. It was an odd sensation. Many students and faculty alike ran to me, embraced me, hugged me, and told me how happy they were that I was back.

The students' eyes filled with tears when I walked into my first class that morning. I remember the uncertainty on their faces. They didn't know how to react. A lot of them cried and were full of emotion. I, too, had tears in my eyes each class that first day. I was happy to see the kids because I loved them so much and, by the same token, I knew that they loved me. Students were yelling out, "Coach, we are so happy to see you. Thanks for coming back. We need you. You have to see the subs they sent in to take your place. They were no Coach Petro." Little did they know how much I needed them. It was an emotional first two weeks back as we all showed our love. As time went on, I cherished working at the school more than ever.

But, every day for months, when I left the school driving back to the Dorsetts' house, I knew Ava would not be waiting for me. As best I could, I tried to get back into a routine. I needed to take my mind off the loneliness. I needed to keep busy with positive things instead of dwelling on my own hurt and sorrow. All the memories at the Dorsett house were with Ava.

Christmas was coming. I saw the decorations everywhere. I heard Christmas carols on the radio and in all the stores. The malls were buzzing with Christmas spirit. This would be my first Christmas without Ava. These holidays were more difficult to deal with because they were the first without baby.

I had to do my Christmas shopping. The family helped with most of it because I wasn't in any mood to do it by myself. I kept thinking about the stores Ava would go to. I was touched as I began going through our stuff. Ava had already bought my presents back in October; a new navy blue sweater and shirt from the Gap still in the bag, along with a bottle of my favorite cologne, Paco Rabanne—another special thing I could hold on to. We both loved to buy things for each other. She always lit up like a child when I brought her presents. In her absence, I just couldn't get into the Christmas spirit. I had no holiday cheer, no sense of anticipation or excitement, knowing that, without her, it would all be fake happiness. The presents she bought me gave me a little sense of our tradition. She wasn't with me, but her presence was.

I flew to New York to spend Christmas in Brooklyn with my family. Everybody says there's no place like New York for the holidays. Usually I would agree, but I could've been anywhere in the world that year, and it wouldn't have made a difference. Without Ava, it was going to be a difficult holiday. Ava loved New York at Christmastime. There's no place on earth like New York during the holiday season. The energy and excitement are awesome. The whole atmosphere of celebration and anticipation is in the air.

My family tried their best to cheer me up on Christmas Eve and make it happy for me. I felt bad for them because they tried so hard not to mention things that would remind me of Ava. Christmas Day wasn't much better. Despite the fact that we were all together and had each other, they knew I was hurting, and they hurt with me. Sometimes love hurts.

I called Mr. and Mrs. D. on Christmas Day. They were at Meemaw's house in Kingwood, Texas, and I could tell it was a somber Christmas for them, too. They said they had gone to the cemetery earlier to visit Ava's grave. I had gone to the cemetery a lot myself. I went on weekdays—weekends—all the time. I put flowers on her grave and screamed to her, "Ava, why did you have to leave me. I didn't want you to go."

New Year's Day 1986 came and went in New York without much fanfare. I felt like a nomad that day, a wanderer, wandering from house to house, spending time with different friends and families, not really feeling comfortable anywhere, but going just the same. It was an empty feeling. I didn't belong anywhere I went. Everyone tried very, very hard; but I had a hollow, empty feeling of loneliness. It's one thing to be lonely and be by yourself. It's worse to be with a lot of people and still feel lonely. That's the loneliest feeling of all.

The next months were excruciatingly sad ones for me. It was hard to imagine going into 1986 without her. I went to the mall by myself. I watched couples walk hand in hand as Ava and I had used to do. It hurt to watch so many happy couples together. Where was my happiness? No one was holding my hand. No one was walking with me. I ate in the food court—by myself. I visited our favorite restaurants—by myself: Casa Ole, El Chico's, and many of the other Mexican restaurants that we loved so well. I went to the stores we had frequented: Target, Miller's Outpost, The Gap, Sam's Club, the Christian music and book stores.

For the first time since we had been married, I was going to all of these places alone. We had loved to stop by Chick-Fil-A for a chicken sandwich and waffle fries. We had loved going to the beach, even in the wintertime. We had taken rides down to Galveston to enjoy the peace and quiet of the water. As we walked along the shore, the sun would just be coming up over the Gulf of Mexico, the waves would be crashing and the sea gulls hovering for food, squawking and carrying on.

Going to church was difficult, also, so I went infrequently. I was confused, hurt, angry, and frustrated—confused that God had allowed this to happen—not that He caused it, but why He didn't stop it; in pain over being alone and having to start over; angry because I had done nothing to deserve this kind of tragedy; and frustrated that I was in a situation that I had no control over. Ava and I had been active with the youth in our church. Seeing the young people and other church friends only reminded me of her, and of the wonderful times we had spent there.

I was experiencing the biggest roller coaster of emotions in my life, knowing I am not a fan of the roller coaster. There are two ways to ride it. One, hold on for dear life, or two, throw your hands up, and see where it will take you. I did things to try to find happiness, then searched once again for something else to help me through the next period of loneliness. Some people say that grief is a day-by-day experience. It wasn't like that for me. It wasn't even a minute-by-minute kind of thing. For me it was a second-by-second battle to try and understand why this had happened to me. I constantly wondered if I was going to continue with my life. The thought, *Will I ever live again?*, kept playing continually in my head.

I kept a journal of my feelings and thoughts. For instance, Valentine's Day 1986 was one of my worst days. While others were celebrating the joys of love in their lives, my love was dead, gone, and buried. How could I enjoy this Valentine's Day? Here are words that culminated my feelings of the time.

January and February were tough months. I wrote these words, on February 25, 1986:

> Today marks four months since my baby has gone. The hurt becomes more real with each passing day. God, help me to find acceptance in this crazy situation. My love for Ava is greater than ever, though I don't have her here with me. God, ease this pain that is so physical in nature. Comfort me in this time of loneliness. Since Valentine's Day, the pain has been sharper. Why, God, has she gone away? Was it my fault? Please be so real to me, for I need You more than ever.
>
> Today was such a beautiful day. The beginning of spring is so evident. These were special times for me and Ava. Lord, as spring brings forth such natural beauty (since winter's cold is ending), please let your beauty illuminate me during this time of anguish. Help me, Lord, for I truly love You. I picked this book [my journal] because of the beauty it displays [a beach scene on the cover]. We truly loved the beach. Oh, how I miss being on the beach with her. The tears roll down my face—they pour from my heart. God, have You betrayed me? Why am I deserted and left alone? I need You, Lord.

The toughest times were at night. I couldn't sleep. I began to have panic and anxiety attacks. I would wake up in a cold sweat, my heart pounding so hard that I thought I would have a heart attack. This scared me because I thought I was too young to have heart problems. I didn't understand what was going on. I did realize that, emotionally and psychologically, it was an uphill battle.

Each one of us was going through many of the same feelings. Mr. D., Mrs. D., and Randa were all feeling anguish, doubt, anger, and guilt. Whenever a tragedy like this happens, it's natural for everyone close to that person to feel a sense of responsibility. "What did I do to cause this to happen to Ava?" "How could I have prevented this tragedy?" "Should we have moved into the house in the first place?" "Why is this happening to our family?" Each one of us wanted answers. None of us could understand why.

My lowest point was reached on March 12, 1986. This would have been our third wedding anniversary. What a way to celebrate a special day. I had been keeping a calendar of days since Ava's death and knew the exact number of days—the hours—even down to the minute; four months, fifteen days, fourteen hours, and twenty-five minutes had passed since Ava had died—what a way to celebrate my anniversary.

I sat in the car and didn't get out. I yelled from the distance at her grave. "Ava, why did you leave me? Please, you still could come back. It's never too late." It seemed like eternity passed as I continually begged her to come back. Slowly, I walked to her burial place. I stood over her grave and stared at her name on the tombstone and the epitaph that read, "She touched her world for Jesus." After a few minutes I placed a bouquet of yellow and purple irises on the stone, right over the date that she died. Irises were her favorite. She loved them so much that they were our wedding flowers. Where were all these tears coming from, I was sobbing more than any other day. I felt the greatest degree of loneliness, despair, anguish, and hurt. Even though I believed she was in a better place, the pain was still excruciating. I'm missing her more than words can say because she was more than just my wife, she was my best friend. Since October 25, this day was the worst of the worst—wondering if I would ever experience joy again—the real, honest, deep-down wonderful joy that makes you feel strong inside—the joy that wells up from your soul and springs forth like a fountain. That's the joy that I missed—the joy I longed for.

CHAPTER

12

Beginning to
See the Light

It became increasingly evident that it would take a long time to work through my grief for the healing to take place. I would have to take it ten seconds at a time, minute by minute, day by day, week by week.

One phone call during my bleakest period really helped me. It came from Nancy Pearson, a friend from Oral Roberts University who now taught in the Houston area. Nancy had been at the wedding, and she had come to the funeral.

"Bobby, I've known you for a while—since 1980," she said. "You have always been someone whom I and many other people looked to as somebody with a lot of strength, somebody with a lot of confidence, a strong faith, a lot of joy—someone who so obviously loves to live. You care about life. You enjoy life. You live life to the fullest. You were always there for others and always listened to others. You are somebody who was always strong for other people."

Then she said, "Bobby, stop it! You've been trying to put on an act. You're trying to be strong for everybody—trying to show everyone that this is not going to get you down—that this is not going to destroy you. And I believe you are going to make it through this, Bobby. But we know you are hurting—we know you're in pain. *Let us help you. Let us strengthen you.* Just like the pastor said at the funeral, we want to uphold *you*, we want to hold up *your* arms, we want to strengthen *you* through this situation… "

When Nancy shared that with me, a burden was lifted. She was right. I didn't have to try and pretend that I was strong. I didn't have to keep up the façade that this wasn't going to get the best of me. I was now free to be honest with people and let them know that, yes, I hurt, yes, I was discouraged, yes, I needed my arms lifted for me, and yes, I needed to vent my emotions. I no longer had to be afraid to discuss my problems with people. I now felt a freedom and a release that I, in fact, had a choice in deciding which direction this tragedy was going to go. Was I going to let this tragedy get the best of me? Or was I going to get the best of this tragedy?

I now saw that it was my choice. God knows what we need and when we need it. That call from Nancy was a turning point in dealing realistically with Ava's death. The conversation triggered in my memory principles that I had learned while taking graduate courses in counseling and psychology at the University of Houston. These principles had been introduced by Elizabeth Kubler Ross in her book *On Death and Dying*. It suddenly hit me that I had been going through all of the stages of grief: denial, anger, shock, depression, bargaining, and acceptance—all except one. I was in denial, because both shock and refusal to accept the fact that the tragedy had taken place had settled in. I was angry with Ava for deserting me, at God for taking her away, and at myself for things that I could've or should've done. I was "shoulding" on myself—pondering things I thought I "should've" done that would have changed the outcome of what actually happened. I bargained with God, saying, "If you'll bring her back, then I'll... " Guilt ran through my veins: What had I done wrong to cause this to happen? Depression came like a blanket of darkness—I was extremely lonely when the reality that she was really gone set in.

I slipped in and out of each stage—except for the one termed "acceptance." It was now time for me to start a new beginning. My healing only began when I accepted that she wasn't coming back. I said "Goodbye" to Ava, and started anew.

This was a critical part of the healing process. I now knew that it was all right to talk about my true feelings. I could share with people how much pain I had gone through in the various surgeries. I could talk about Ava and what she meant to me. I went to the cemetery and to other secluded places and vented my anger—often yelling and screaming at the top of my lungs. I expressed to God my hurt, my confusion, and my pain.

I was no longer afraid to cry if I felt the need to do so. This was a real release for me. Just as Nancy had said, I didn't need to pretend to be strong for anyone. I felt like crying, I needed to cry, so I cried.

I read articles and literature about death. It was a comfort to get different perspectives from other people who had been traumatized by a death. Andre Thornton, a professional baseball player with the Cleveland Indians, had tragically lost his wife and daughter in a van accident. Reading about how Andre dealt with his loss, trusted in his faith, and battled his way through, inspired me. I read about Dave Roever, a Navy SEAL in the Vietnam War. A phosphorous grenade had blown up in his hand. He lived through it but was severely injured. He fought back and has impacted many lives.

Another person who inspired me was Terry Law. Terry started a ministry called Living Sound. Living Sound worked abroad, traveling throughout Russia and other parts of the world sharing love, hope, and God with people who desperately needed this message. While Terry was in Europe with his group, his wife was killed in an automobile accident here in the United States. Reading about how he dealt with his loss helped me to identify with someone who had gone through something similar to what I was experiencing.

Instead of going to a particular counselor, I was able to vent my feelings with family and close friends. My friend Jay, who was working on his master's degree in counseling and psychology, helped me recognize the things that I needed to deal with. As time went on, it became easier for me to move forward in a positive direction. I was no longer afraid to spend time alone. I didn't like it, but it didn't eat at me as much now.

I kept some special things of Ava's so that I could remember the good times and not try to act as if they didn't still mean a lot to me. I kept her wedding ring, her watch, earrings, clothing, and pictures. I also kept myself busy, especially with my students.

I volunteered with youth organizations like Students Against Drunk Driving and the Fellowship of Christian Athletes group, which I sponsored at Santa Fe. I spent more time with the kids individually and in small groups, taking them to ball games, concerts, and other activities that we had fun doing together. I knew that I had been spared so that I could someday share with young people about the dangers of drinking and driving.

I started to exercise and feel better about myself. I still felt self-conscious about my numerous scars and the permanent blemishes on my body, but I was getting back into shape and feeling more confident about my appearance. I was recording more than ever my feelings and frustrations in the journal. This helped me to have a positive outlet. Finally, I had to turn my grief into creative energy by helping others, knowing that by helping others in need, I would be helping myself.

I was looking at life differently now. I had a new perspective. I knew my life was spared for a reason—some greater purpose and calling. I could have been in a wheelchair for the rest of my life. It has been said that some always have it worse than what you are dealing with. I could have had brain damage. I could have been injured worse than I was. Yes, I had had difficult surgeries, and yes, I had been severely injured, but it could've been much worse. I now had learned to look at the positive aspects of my circumstances instead of dwelling on the negatives and letting them weigh me down and keep me down.

I learned the importance of a little thing called attitude. I realized more than ever that I had the power to change my attitude and develop a positive outlook. I began to listen to uplifting and positive music. I started watching more comedies on television. I watched *I Love Lucy*, *Abbott and Costello*, and *The Little Rascals*. This influx of comedy and funny programs helped to bring joy back to my life. I had learned how to laugh again. Just months earlier, I hadn't been sure if I would be able to.

Venting my emotions was so important. Whether it was talking, crying, praying, shouting, laughing, singing, praising, rejoicing, or whatever—I had to get my emotions out in any way I could. Sometimes I did all of the above, one right after the other. It gave me a needed sense of release. There were too many different feelings that I had to get out of my system. It was wonderful to be free enough to just let go.

One way I was able to experience a sense of release was by watching *Rocky* films, starring Sylvester Stallone. The original *Rocky* had always been one of my favorite movies. It's the story of a boxer, Rocky Balboa, a loser from the streets of Philadelphia who gets a once-in-a-lifetime shot at the heavyweight championship. He goes the distance with the champion and never gives up. Despite all kinds of adversity and hardship, Rocky triumphs over impossible odds. I identified with Rocky because he was just a down-and-out guy fighting for his life.

The 1980 miracle USA Olympic hockey team inspired me. They beat the Soviets and went on to win the gold medal against Finland. It was another real life David and Goliath. I realized more than ever after talking to Nancy that I was going to have to make a choice. This situation was either going to make me a better person, or it was going to make me a bitter person. I could let this tragedy be the controller or I could control it. It was time for my foundational principles to kick in.

One film that came out several years after Ava's death really hit home with me. *The Money Pit,* starring Shelley Long and Tom Hanks, is about an engaged couple fixing up an old home to move into when they are married. This movie never gave Tom Hanks much recognition, but it had an awesome story line. As the story goes, the house completely falls apart. The bathtub crashes through the floor, the fireplace collapses, the staircase breaks, the walls come apart, the electrical and plumbing systems are a complete mess. The house is a disaster. It's a comedy and it's funny. As the movie goes on, the couple's relationship also comes apart mirroring the house. As they are on the verge of splitting up, the contractor—who has fixed the home so that it is absolutely gorgeous—walks down the staircase he has just finished. Tom

Hanks is on one side of the foyer and Shelley Long is on the other. The contractor, who is all too aware of their differences, lays the key to the house on the banister and asks, "Who gets the key?" He continues by telling them he had doubts whether the house could be fixed, but in the end he knew that it could because it had a strong foundation. He says, "No matter how bad a house may be, if it has a strong foundation, then it can be fixed." He wasn't only talking about the house, but about their relationship. He knew their relationship had a strong foundation.

That struck me—the strong foundation. No matter what happens—no matter how bad, how bleak, how dark, how desolate a situation may seem—it can always be put back together if there is a strong foundation.

This was reaffirmed to me after witnessing the devastation left by Hurricane Andrew in Miami in August 1992. Even now in 2005, this is the costliest hurricane in American history. A three-day cruise turned into a five-day adventure because our ship could not sail into the Miami port during the storm. When we finally returned, the destruction was catastrophic; total housing areas lay in ruin and lives were left in chaos. The only thing left intact in the midst of the devastation were row after row of concrete foundations from flattened houses. I realized then that no matter how much destruction the storm had caused, the homes could be rebuilt on that solid foundation. If our foundations in life are strong, then even when the hurricanes of life come calling, our foundation will be left intact and we can always rebuild our lives.

We can rely on a strong foundation, rebuild a poor foundation, or start building a new foundation. It's never too late. It's one decision, ten seconds away. My life, too, could be put back together. My foundation is strong. It will be difficult—knowing that any good thing in life comes out of pain, loss, rejection, and tragedy. But it's how we respond—it's not how many times you get knocked down, but your willingness to get back up. The difference between success and failure is one decision. Those who succeed and those who fail, both fall down just as much. The difference is—the person who succeeds is willing to get up one more time. Life will have pain. How we respond to that pain can determine our success or failure. Pain is inevitable, but suffering is optional!

CHAPTER

13

Give Faith a Fighting Chance

Building a strong foundation comes down to making one choice—one decision at a time. Each decision has the power to not only affect us, but also others. This takes place one situation at a time: Brick by brick, row by row, layer by layer—one ten-second decision at a time—whether it's a good decision or a bad decision. That's how we build our foundation. The point we're at right now in our lives was reached by making one ten-second decision at a time. Our past defines who we are today. Good or bad; right or wrong—the patterns and routines are set little by little. Our habits influence our personalities and also our lives.

Faith was established in my life when I was very young. My family attended church regularly, and I learned Christian principles. From those principles, I became interested in a Christian university. It was a step-by-step progression, an outgrowth of what I had been taught when I was a child. The formative years in children are perhaps the most important ones in our lives. Those are the years that can determine the path our lives will take. Will we follow a right path? Or will we follow another path? The establishment of faith in my life had been an important element in my formative years. Faith is what we believe and put our hope in. What we believe in becomes our security. It's how we respond even when we can't see the end in sight. Faith can be described as believing—even when you don't understand or have all the answers. Faith is not always being right. We all fall down and make mistakes.

There are three kinds of faith: First, there is a faith in a Supreme Being, a faith in a religion, a faith in God. My faith is grounded in being a follower of Jesus Christ. His example of unconditional love is the greatest precedent that has been set. Second, there is the faith to believe in yourself—to believe that, somehow, some way, you can work to make the best of every situation and that you will ultimately get the best of it. It's knowing that you have the ability to get through any situation you may face. Your personal value propels you either forward or back. A third kind of faith is having a belief in others— relying on the wisdom they have gained from their own experiences. We are here to help each other. The greatest success is what we do to help others to overcome and fulfill their destinies. We all fall down, and we can teach others how to get up. Living and learning will allow us to pick others up in their time of need. When faced with tragedy, we go to our sources: God, self and others.

A tragedy can steer people in two directions: It can control us, or we can control *it*. We have to make the conscious choice to have faith. Once we recognize that we have the power to choose the right path, then we can make the choice to be on the way to a better life.

I define faith in such a case by rejecting the norm. The norm would say, "This has happened to you, so you're going to have to be bitter, you're going to have to be hateful, you must be unforgiving, you must not love." Well, I had to choose to reject those negative feelings from the start. I had to choose to go against what society tells me. I would not let myself buckle under the pressure of grief.

The second part of my faith is a knowing that somehow I would make it through this situation. Even in the dictionary, *faith* is defined as "a belief without evidence, and a confidence in, or dependence on a person; belief in God." I had a knowing deep down in my spirit that no matter how difficult things might seem, no matter how tragic that the circumstances might be, I was going to make it through. I knew God would always make a way. He says to cast all your cares upon Him, for He cares for you (see 1 Peter 5:7). The whole Christian faith and belief system is not built on what society says and does, but on a belief that God will be our source of help. Christians aren't always the best examples. Much hatred has been shed in the name of God. He doesn't work through control, fear, manipulation, judgment, condemnation and guilt. He is our comforter and safe place.

It's not about what we want, but that He knows what we need. We have to do our part, but we also have to make the choice to allow Him to work through us and others. He won't force Himself on us. We must invite Him in. He didn't send the tragedy, but His greatest desire is to turn it into triumph. He wants good to come out of bad as others are also helped to revive their faith.

Mel Gibson's 2004 blockbuster, *The Passion of the Christ*, depicts what Christ did for us. He overcame sin, adversity, temptation, but most of all, He overcame death itself. If we believe that He overcame death, then why can't we believe that He will help us overcome anything that stands in our way? He wants to help us—and He will. All we have to do is ask and believe. He is ready and willing to be with us every step of the way, but first we have to recognize that we need His help.

I also believe that "faith without works is dead" (James 2:26). In other words, are we willing to put our money where our mouths are? It's easy to follow God and do what's right when things are going well, but what happens when things go wrong or we face difficulties? Will we just lie down and give up? This was a time that I had to stand strong on my foundation. This was a situation that truly defined my faith. I had to believe that faith in God would see me through.

People have asked me, "Don't you think that God could've steered the truck six inches to the left or six inches to the right? That way the accident would not have been fatal." It's probably true that the truck's impact six inches one way or the other would have meant a difference in life and death for Ava. But that did not happen.

The driver of the pickup made a choice. He chose to drink. He chose to drive. In the ten seconds it took for him to lose control of his truck, my life was changed, my wife's life was taken, his life was changed—all because he made the wrong choice. He had reacted from the foundation he had laid for himself. We have all prepared to succeed or to fail.

There's an expression, "Actions speak louder than words." It's true. What you do speaks louder than any words you can ever say. I could've said, "Yes, I believe that God will help me through this," then sat back and done nothing. Or I could've said, "Yes, God will help me through this," and got out there and moved forward with my life and *allowed* Him to work through what I was doing. That's what I chose.

I get angry with people who sit around and mope, saying, "I need direction. I need guidance. God needs to tell me what to do next." Then they sit around, do nothing, and expect God to speak audibly to them about what their next move should be. I don't believe God works that way. If we don't know what to do next, we should get out there and start doing things that we think He wants us to do. He'll make it clear one way or the other which direction He wants us to go. We make the choice, and then God directs our path. Take that first step. Choose to have faith.

I heard a story of a man whose house was flooded in a rainstorm. This man got on top of his roof to wait out the storm and avoid the rising waters. A short time later a man in a four-wheel-drive vehicle came by and yelled up to him. "Sir, come down. We're here to rescue you." The man on the roof called down, "Thanks, but I'll be all right. God will take care of me. He will deliver me." So the vehicle drove off and left him.

A few hours later, when the water was so high that no cars could pass, a man came by in a boat. "Hey, mister, get in the boat. I'm here to rescue you." The man on the roof said, "No. God's going to rescue me." The man in the boat looked puzzled but moved on.

Later in the afternoon, the flood waters rose so high that they reached the man's roof. A helicopter flew over, the pilot dropped a ladder, and spoke through the loudspeaker. "Hey, you on the roof. Grab the ladder. I'm here to rescue you."

"Oh, no. Thanks, anyway. I'll stay here. I'm trusting in God. He's going to rescue me," the man said. The helicopter pilot reluctantly left. The water rose again and the man on the roof drowned. When he arrived in heaven, he asked God, "What happened? I trusted you. I had faith. Why did you let me drown?"

God said, "Save you? I sent you a Jeep, a boat, and a helicopter to rescue you. You were too busy thinking I was going to move and meet your needs in a certain way, instead of realizing that I was setting a way of escape for you!"

God provides different ways of escape for us. They may not be exactly what we want them to be, but who knows better, us or God? He will always provide for us. It may not be in the manner that we think, but He will take care of us.

I went to the cemetery on our third wedding anniversary. I went to Ava's grave site and laid flowers at her grave. I talked to her and asked her why had she left me alone. I was angry with her and angry at God for allowing this to happen. I started to yell at God and cry out to Him because I couldn't believe that He would allow this to happen and then make me face this situation all alone.

"God, You could have stopped this," I prayed in anger. "I always believed and trusted in You—now I feel so all alone. I need You because the hurt I'm feeling is unbearable. I need Your help—I can't handle it alone," I said.

Ava and I had always loved Him and trusted Him. Why had He let us down? Why was He not comforting me? I was so angry that I threw the Bible down and screamed for several minutes.

Finally, I was so distraught that I fell down on my knees and prayed out loud, "God, I can't do this alone. I've been hurting for four months now. I need to know that You're with me. I feel like You've abandoned me. Please show me that You love me. Please give me a sign that You'll always be with me and never forsake me. If I am going to continue in life without Ava, and continue to serve You, I need to know more than ever that You are going to be with me.

"I'm willing to go through life without Ava. But I'm not willing to go through life feeling that You are not with me. I understand that I have to work through the pain, but I need to know You are with me."

All of a sudden—out of nowhere—I felt warm arms wrap around me. I thought that someone in the cemetery had heard me crying and yelling, and had come over and put their arms around me to comfort me. I was hesitant and embarrassed to open my eyes and see who it was, so I squinted one eye open to take a peak at who was hugging me. I looked around and I realized that, physically, there was no one there.

God was saying to me that He was always going to be there—because He loved me. This was a turning point. It marked a change in my heart. I now saw and had actually felt first hand that God had something special planned for my life. I came away with a new attitude. God had revealed Himself to me that day. I knew God's grace and mercy would sustain me. My life was changed for the better. I knew that I would conquer and overcome this tragedy. My faith was a shield—a protector against any thoughts of doubt and despair. Like a knight in battle, I had to carry my faith before me. God's ultimate goal is for restoration to take place.

The faith that had been established as a young child was coming back to sustain and guide me in this time that I needed it most. Faith had proved to be the cornerstone of my foundation. This is what this house of mine is built on. It was rooted for such a time as this.

CHAPTER

14

Forgiveness Is Optional

I had only been in the hospital for a short time that fateful night when the word came to me from Mr. and Mrs. Dorsett that the driver who had crashed through our house and killed Ava had been drunk. This couldn't be so. I'd done so much with my students to work against this. I had constantly told my students about the danger, the irresponsibility, and the ignorance a person displays by driving while intoxicated. This couldn't be true. It was too ironic, after all that I'd done to fight against such behavior.

Why was this happening to me? Ava's death was a tragedy—and knowing that a drunk driver had killed her made it worse. This tragedy could have been prevented. The pain was severe; my body felt as if it were on fire. Ava was dead, and I had to hear news like this. Why? Why had this happened? The irresponsibility and actions of this one man, which had changed the lives of many, was the result of a poor ten-second decision. Our patterns of decision making catch up with us—we prepare to succeed and we prepare to fail.

I now found out that he had been drinking for almost the entire day. I was told that he had had problems at work and had spent the major part of the day barhopping. He wasn't just a little intoxicated—he was grossly intoxicated. His blood alcohol content was .19. Estimates were that the driver had the equivalent of fifteen beers in a two-hour period when he got into his truck and tried to drive home. If he had been drinking throughout the day, why didn't someone stop him? If he was with friends, why didn't they stop him? Where were the bartenders? Couldn't they see the condition he was in?

All the feelings of anger and frustration, bitterness and hatred, by this time had reached a boiling point. What would I have done if I got my hands on this guy? Would I wring his neck? The Bible says, "An eye for an eye, a tooth for a tooth," right?

Inside my spirit, something was asking, "Bobby, have you forgotten what you believe? You were brought up in a Christian home and were taught to forgive. Your whole Christian faith is based on forgiveness. That is why Jesus died on the cross—to forgive sinners."

I said to God, "But, God, this man was a drunk driver. He killed my wife. He shouldn't be forgiven. Are you telling me that I have to forgive him?"

I realized now that I was going to have to make a choice and choose to forgive. It wasn't just going to happen because of my faith in God. I had to make a conscious choice to forgive and to *decide* to do it. This was not going to be easy. It was going to be one of the toughest things I'd ever had to do. As I lay in bed in the hospital after Ava had been dead for only a few hours, I remember praying this prayer:

"Father, I know that I have learned and have been taught since I was a child that I need to forgive those who've wronged me. Christianity is based on forgiveness, and I know the importance of forgiveness to You. God, I know that what I am going to have to deal with and what I'll have to do will be the most difficult thing I have ever had to do in my life. I need Your help and Your strength to do this. I know You want me to forgive this man. But without You, I cannot do this on my own. I now make a choice that I will work at forgiving this man because I also know that if I am going to make it through this tragedy and find healing, I need to forgive."

Now when I say forgive the man, I don't mean that he should walk away scot-free. Justice needs to be served. The driver of the pickup was supposed to serve at least eighteen to thirty-six months of a ten-year involuntary manslaughter sentence—too light a sentence, I thought. Sadly, I later found out that he served only four months in jail. He should have served more time. Justice was not carried out. But the point was—I had to forgive. Forgiving him didn't mean that I was letting him off the hook or condoning his behavior. It didn't mean it was okay that he had killed Ava, either. It didn't mean that he shouldn't have to pay back something to society. He should have had to pay a price, some kind of price. Breaking the law should cost something. We have the freedom of choice—but not the freedom of consequence.

But I had to forgive him for *my* sake, so that I could be free—free from hatred—free from bitterness—free from the bondage that could enslave me for the rest of my life unless I released my anger so I could begin to heal. When we don't forgive, we are taking ownership of that person's problem, and I have enough to deal with without adding someone else's issues to mine. God showed me that He wouldn't be able to fully work in my life until I was willing to fully forgive this man.

Just because I prayed that prayer that night while lying in the hospital bed, and I chose to forgive, didn't mean that forgiveness would happen automatically or overnight. Forgiveness is a continual process. It takes a choice—not an easy one. It's ten seconds at a time—one step at a time—one day at a time. But in the end, it's worth it all. I would not be where I am today if I had not chosen to forgive. Unforgiveness is like drinking poison and hoping the person who offended you is hurt from the poison you drink. It's allowing the pain of the past to stay active and present. Looking at our past with unforgiveness inhibits us from fulfilling our future. It hinders and clouds our minds. It's like the offender is attached to you and you drag him with you. It's spending all your driving time looking in the rearview mirror. When we don't forgive, we are telling others we are perfect and never make mistakes.

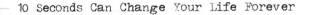

This is the furthest thing from the truth. Maybe if I reacted to my pain in this way negatively, I could have been in his shoes. Maybe a few more bad decisions in my life could have led me to do the same thing. I may not have driven drunk through someone's house, but I have done my share of hurting others. Pain breeds pain. I can promise you, this man had unresolved issues—we all do. And he probably had unforgiveness in his heart. That is why grace and mercy become some of our greatest gifts. Forgiving others, even when they have done nothing to deserve our forgiveness is the key. Wow! How incredible is that! Remember you have hurt others and desperately want to be forgiven. With all the pain and loneliness that I was feeling, another straw would have broken the camel's back. If I didn't forgive him, the bitterness would hold me back, and there would be no moving forward in my life. If I didn't work at forgiving this man, he would tragically affect me a second time. First, in taking Ava's life; second, in my not being able to move on with my life and make the best of my situation.

Too many people believe—and they believe this strongly—that by holding a grudge over someone and not forgiving them, they somehow have control, even to the point of putting a "curse" over that person. In this manner they feel that they are getting back at the person. When people hold unforgiveness inside themselves, they are not punishing the other person— they are hurting themselves. The anger and resentment will eat away at them like a slow poison. Slowly. Surely.

Is this the way to live? To repay evil with evil? Think of what kind of world we would have if everyone repaid evil with evil. Unfortunately, with the problems of drugs and guns in many places, this is an alarming reality. Many gangs are instilling hatred and fear in communities with this principle of evil for evil—that's wrong.

At times I thought I couldn't go on. If I had chosen not to forgive this man, it would have pushed me over the edge. Think what would have happened if I had said, "Okay, buddy. You ruined my life. Now I'm going to ruin yours," and then proceeded to hound him or threaten his family, or do some other vengeful thing. In one sense, I had every right to be angry. But if I had taken the law into my own hands and done something foolish to repay this man with evil, I myself would now be in jail, and that would have been a double tragedy.

Ava always used to say to me, "Remember, we are not responsible for how others act toward us or how they treat us, but we are responsible for our actions, reactions, and responses toward them." We take offense because we take ownership of other people's actions. Our own insecurity does this. "There must be something wrong with me—that's why this happened." We end up viewing ourselves as wrong beings because of the wrongs of others.

Don't let unforgiveness be a roadblock in your life. It can immobilize you—like a flat tire on a car without a spare. If there's a person or persons or a situation that is keeping you from being the person that God wants you to be, go to that person privately, write them a note, or—if it's too difficult yet to do that—make sure you do your part by forgiving that person. I guarantee that you will feel a huge burden lifted off you. You'll feel as if you can jump over the moon. The chains and bondage that held you hostage will be gone. Now you will be able to move forward with your life and live with freedom. We tend to judge others by their actions and ourselves by our motives. We need to be more sensitive of others.

It's always something. There are always things to deal with. That's just it, there are things. When it's all said and done though, what matters? When my life is over, was it worth it to hold so many grudges? I remember speaking to a loss recovery group. There happened to be an elderly woman that was directly affected from the concentration camps of World War II. After my program was over she came up to talk with me. I could see the pain in her face. "I will never forgive those Nazi's for killing my family; no way." My heart broke. She has carried this pain for sixty years. You can't tell me she hasn't let this hinder her life?

Let forgiveness be a major part of your life foundation. Choose to forgive today. Better yet, choose not to be so easily offended. If you are not offended, then you have nothing to forgive. Don't let the poison in. You *can* make that choice—but only you can do it. Love is the greatest gift of all. Part of that love is learning how to give and receive forgiveness. When it's all been said and done, there is just one thing that matters: Did I live my life for truth? What I've done for love's reward will stand the test of time. Offenses are inevitable. Forgiveness is optional!

CHAPTER 15

Family and Friends

A ctions speak louder than words. I cannot say it often enough. When a tragedy such as Ava's death happens, you see how important your family and friends are. You also get to see who your true friends are. They love you no matter what—no conditons—when you look, act, and are your best and worst. This becomes clearer by way of how much strength and support you draw from them. It means the world to be embraced by their support and unconditional love—not answers, just support.

I'll never forget when my mother and older sister, Debbie, first walked into my hospital room. As they saw me all banged up, they wept uncontrollably. My mom's first words to me were, "Bobby, I remember when you were a little boy. I could always make the pain go away or help you feel better. But I feel

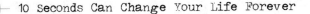

helpless now because I can't take this pain away from you. If I could, I would. You are going to have to work through this. Just know that I will do all I can to help you." It has to be difficult for a parent to see their kids in this condition. Now as a parent I feel the hurt, when my kids hurt. You never want to see them struggle, especially like this.

My sister Debbie wrote about how she felt—seeing me for that first time since the tragedy:

> When I walked into the hospital room and saw my brother lying in the bed, covered with blood and bandages, I dropped my suitcase and threw myself across him. My mother did the same. We all sobbed together—racking sobs, straight from the depths of our souls. I knew that I have never felt such anguish and devastation. At that moment I wished that my baby brother had perished along with his beloved wife, so that he would not have to be left here on earth to suffer without her.
>
> "Oh God, I will gladly take his grief upon myself. I can't bear to see him suffer."

Later that same day, Debbie, Mom, and Mrs. D. went to look at my house for the first time since the tragedy. These were words that Debbie used to describe the scene:

> We walked (me, Mom, Linda Dorsett) into the house at night with a flashlight. I was shocked. It looked like a hurricane had hit this once lovely home. We stumbled over plaster, brick, shattered glass, wood, pieces of furniture and belongings, dust, and debris. The wind whistled and flapped through the heavy black plastic that covered the huge hole that was once the bedroom wall. The feeling was eerie. Doom and despair shivered through my body. I tried hard not to re-create the moment of impact in my mind. I had to get out of there. It was like being in a nightmare or horror movie. Tears sprang from my eyes and I couldn't breathe.
>
> I'll never forget that sight, and that feeling, the smell—etched in my mind forever.

My mother had left her job and ended up staying with me for the entire three weeks that I was in the hospital. She knew what her priorities were. Debbie, who at the time had a four-year-old son, Nicholas, dropped everything to come and be with me; first, for the funeral and then, for my first week in the hospital. We've always been a very tight family, and this confirmed to me more than ever how much having a loving and caring family meant. Being there in any way—without being asked—is essential.

My mother stayed with me—by my side for fifteen hours a day while I was in the hospital and going through my various surgeries. She stayed by my bedside from morning 'til night. I had to force her to go back to the Dorsett's house where she was staying. She didn't want to leave me. Knowing that she was with me so many hours each day gave me a comfort that I cannot express.

Debbie was able to be with me for a week and a half before she had to go back to New York. She did all that she could to cheer me up—there were even moments when she made me laugh. Reminiscing about the old times can bring joy to an otherwise bleak situation.

My younger sister, Chrissy (Chrisi, Chrissi, Crisi, Crissi-depending on how she chooses to spell it on any given day), was eighteen at this time. When Ava and I were married, Chrissy had been fifteen and had her personal issues with Ava—Ava being from Texas and Chrisi was very much "New York City." I was her big brother. Chrissi, like every sister, was only looking out for my best interests.

Twice that summer before the accident, Crisi had come down to visit Ava and me. It was a great time of growth in the relationship between her and Ava. Crissi had matured and could now see the type of person Ava was, and that she was a wonderful wife for me. So, when Chrissie heard about the accident, she was especially devastated because she had recently grown to really love Ava after several years of misunderstanding. Being happy that they reconciled, she called me from New York and told me that she was so hurt she didn't think she would be able to cope with being at the funeral. It would be too overwhelming to handle. We all seem to have our own issues of guilt when death is involved.

My father called me, crying and despondent. It's not often you hear your dad so hurt and in such despair with the understanding that there was very little he could do. Dad had a major stroke two years earlier and was now confined to a wheelchair. Dads may not always share their feelings in words, but they have their own way of letting you know how much they care. Though Chrissie and Dad were in New York, I knew their spirits were with me. Throughout my entire recovery period, my family did all they could to support me in every way. Even when I was not so lovable to be around, they tolerated my mood swings. They were very understanding. They were also hurt by the fact that, not only did I lose a wife, but they had lost a daughter-in-law and sister-in-law. They, too, had real pain to deal with, individually.

Letters and cards from around the country soon flooded into Friendswood as people heard about the tragedy. I had had no idea how many people loved us until this horrible tragedy occurred. Calls and support from family, friends, and friends of family members came in. I was blown away by the overwhelming response of love and compassion. It not only came from around the country, but around the world. People I didn't know directly were wishing me well and sending their regards. There was a tidal wave of sympathy. Hundreds of people called, sent flowers, and donations.

Ava's parents were great. I knew their pain must have been so heavy on their hearts, but they never ceased to show their love for me, even in the loss of their daughter. It was probably their way of loving Ava through loving me. Mr. D. came to me while I was in the hospital and said to me that he would take care of all the funeral and memorial arrangements. He was so strong that way. This had to be an unbelievably difficult time for both he and Mrs. D. to handle. Ava's parents were with me at the hospital for many hours on end and did all that they could to comfort me, my family, and my friends. On top of that, they would open their home for me to live with them.

Friends also rallied around me when I needed them most. They really proved what love and friendship is all about. Not only did they come down that weekend, but Jay, Joe, and Cheeks also made special trips to visit me while I continued to live and teach in Texas as I was recuperating. One of my fondest memories was how Jakey surprised me for the weekend. He showed up at school and burst into one of my classes.

These are the types of friends I had. They would do anything for me. I realized how important my days at ORU had been—the baseball team, former athletes, and others friends showed incredible support for me during this time. Mike Moore, an ex-ORU teammate who was pitching for the Seattle Mariners, gave travel money to Joe and Chris. Cheeks was living in Pittsburgh and, ironically, had just gotten back from touring New York and Connecticut with a theater company where he was performing in plays against drug and alcohol abuse. He left the production without hesitation. It was the only time I had ever seen him cry.

Toni Swain Fowler, who was Ava's best friend and had also become a close friend of mine, had a younger sister named Alli, who was twenty years old at the time of Ava's death. Over the course of the next year, Alli would eventually die from the disabling effects of cystic fibrosis. After I arrived home from the hospital that first day, Alli gave me this little booklet of poems that she had written titled, "Please Remember… " This meant the world to me because I knew the pain that she was enduring day by day and the incredible courage that she displayed in fighting her disease. Alli's homemade, hand-written booklet contained these words:

Please Remember… That I Love You

I'd like to capture a rainbow
and stick it in a big box
So that anytime you wanted to,
you could reach in and pull it out.
A piece of sunshine.
I'd like to build you a mountain
that you could call your very own—
A place to find serenity
in those times you feel the need
to be closer to yourself.
I'd like to be the one who's there with you
when you're lonely or troubled
or you just need someone to hold onto…
I'd like to do all this and more
to make your life happy
But sometimes it isn't easy to do the things

I would like to do
Or give the things I would like to give.
So… until I learn how to catch rainbows
and build mountains,
Let me do for you which I know best…
Let me simply be your friend.
You are struggling…
I see it
I feel it
I hurt for you.
But I must tell you, dear friend
I believe with all my heart
that you will emerge somehow wiser,
stronger, and more aware.
Hold onto that thought, tuck it away
in the corner of your heart
Until the hurt melts enough for the learning
To have meaning.
I feel inside of me the sadness of your heart
when things aren't going right.
And my eyes, too, filled with tears—
because I know how you feel,
And because I cherish you so very much
and feel so close by your side.
If only I could
I would right the wrongs and make the days brighter
Because I soon want to see the smile I remember
That sparkles so
When things are going well.
There are times when you have been hurt so badly
That you become certain that the pain will never pass.
But it does…
Sometimes because of your efforts
Sometimes in spite of them,

But always,
Always... it goes away.
So, hold on, and know that tomorrow will come
And with each tomorrow... It will be better.
All I have to offer is my love
to remind you that you're not alone
My hand... to hold and to help
My simple words... that time will take you
to a brighter day,
and strength will walk beside you.
And your heart will show the way.

I read these poems often when I needed to be encouraged. They were a source of strength from one so young and so fragile herself who brought confidence to me. I know that I will see her someday. I can't wait to tell her how much she meant to me.

The pastors, staff, and congregations from Lakewood Church and Friendswood United Methodist Church were always present to help, too.

Gary Causey, a friend of mine and vice principal at Santa Fe High School, was at the hospital regularly. He shared with me how my experience was drawing him closer to God. He had a family and other responsibilities, but somehow he made it a priority to be with me. He came to my bedside one night in the hospital, crying, and said, "Remember the night of the accident, when you and I were talking at the football game in Wharton—we were talking about God, and you said that sometimes people make ignorant and irresponsible choices and that they can't blame God? That really hit home to me when this happened to you—and I found out this guy was a drunk driver."

The Ragland Family—Joe, Linda, Shelly, and Joey—had me over to their house for dinner once or twice a week. They took me out with them. We saw the Harlem Globetrotters together. They even took me on a family trip to Colorado to see the Rocky Mountains. They made me feel welcome, loved, and part of their family. They'll never realize in a million years the impact that their compassion had on me. It's exactly what I needed. The Raglands were sent by God—I know they were.

During the entire time immediately after the accident and in the time that I stayed in Texas as I recovered, I saw how absolutely vital my family and friends were to me. One of the reasons that I was able to come through this ordeal as well as I did was because of their constant love and support.

Ava wrote something about friendship that I have saved all these years:

A friend is one with whom you dare to be yourself. And as we share ourselves, we also learn more about ourselves. A friend is someone with whom you can truly share all the important aspects and dimensions of your heart that make you, you—who makes being excited about something so much more delicious as they delight in the pleasure you are experiencing. Someone you can be quiet and mellow with, when you don't feel like talking, but just basking in His presence and tasting His riches. Even though the rest of your world expects you to have it all together—to have all the answers—a friend allows you to be confused, and ask questions, knowing as you seek truth you will find it, and be that much richer in real knowledge. A friend is someone whom you always feel loved by, and know that in your weakness, you are accepted.

She concluded on the back of that piece of college-ruled plain notebook paper:

Live life to the fullest. Get the most from each hour, each day of your life. Then you can look forward with confidence; and back without regrets.

If you were there for me in any way at all, thank you. Thank you times a "gazillion"! God has a way of sending just the right people at just the right time. He knows what you need more than you do.

CHAPTER

16

Growth Is Optional

I n life we all fall down, make mistakes, and miss the mark. Life is filled with adversity, obstacles, and pain. It's always something—par for the course. It is not how many times you fall down, but how many times you are willing to get up. The difference between success and failure is one decision. Those who succeed and those who fail—both fall down just as many times. The difference is: The one who succeeds was willing to get up one more time.

There are so many stories of those who fought through the darkness. Dave Roever (not Rover) was seriously injured in the Vietnam War. For every reason, he should have died. He was burned on most of his body when the phosphorus grenade he was holding in his hand was shot. The agony of facing his wife was overwhelming. "Will she love me? Look at my body, it's a mess! How can I go on living this way." If you've ever heard him speak, you would be amazed. Through his tremendous adversity, he held onto his faith, his hope, and his love. Today, he travels the world helping others. He has been married for almost forty years. His sons now work with him. He tells how when he first saw his wife in his battered condition, he said, "Darling, I'm sorry I can't look good for you." His wife responded, "Davey, you were never good looking anyway." In other words, she was really saying, "I love you for who you are." Dave Roever stresses the importance of how a solid foundation in our lives will *always* see us through. When you think about people like Dave, who have truly overcome adversity and conquered major obstacles in life, you realize they did it by depending on the strength of their own foundation—one that had already been established. Dave tells how life will bring scars, but you can turn them into stars. Triumphant people seem to have some foundational principles in common. They all know that change has occurred, but it's what they do with that change that makes the difference. Their foundations stood firm through the turbulent storms they had to weather—and some have had to weather hurricanes.

W. Mitchell was in several small plane crashes. He now spends his life confined to a wheelchair. His pain has been overwhelming yet he travels the world teaching others how to overcome. His greatest phrase is, "It's not what happens to you, it's what you do about it." In life we can't control everything; pain, rejection, adversity and heartache will come. That's inevitable—they will. What is most important is how we respond to that pain. Our response determines whether we grow or not.

Men like Terry Law (whose wife was killed while he was overseas helping others) and Andre Thornton (former major league baseball star who lost his wife and daughter when their van lost control on an icy patch of road) have truly inspired me. I not only can relate to their depth of pain, but they have also experienced losing a wife, a partner, and love. The common denominators of triumphant people are determination, drive, and a fighting spirit. Many have also relied on faith, family, friends, the willingness to forgive, and love to help them through their difficulties. Their determination is so strong that they will not allow their problems to destroy them. The will, the guts, the motivation to conquer the challenge are all present. There is a desire in a triumphant person to meet the challenge head-on and not be intimidated by the confrontation.

This is as true in sports as it is in life. So much of sports is more psychological than physical. Why does the coach give a pep talk to his team right before they take the field for a game? He knows that on any given day, one team can beat another team. His athletes may not be as physically talented as their opponents are on that day, but if they can believe they can win, play as a team, and execute the plays better than the other team, then they have a better chance to win. Every year in sports there are always upsets in which a David slays a Goliath. You can probably name two or three occasions when that has happened. That's what makes sports so unpredictable. You have to play the game. That's what makes life so exciting—you must prepare to win.

The next time you're watching a basketball game on television, if one team suddenly makes a run of eight or ten consecutive points look at the faces of both teams. One will undoubtedly have the look of defeat or despair, the other will be jubilant and pumped up with enthusiasm and elation. This is the psychological factor that can make or break a game. The coach of the team that is trailing, if he's a good coach, will either call a time-out or find a way to instill confidence in his team so that they never give up. He has to help them to turn the game around—change the momentum—take back control. It's all about the will, the guts, and the motivation. Never, ever give up.

To achieve victory, each of us has to take advantage of one of the greatest gifts of all—freedom of choice. Victory doesn't just happen within a person's life. Careers don't just happen overnight. Movie stars and athletes may seem to suddenly appear as "overnight" successes, but don't kid yourself. You can be sure that those people put in countless, upon countless, upon countless amounts of unseen hours of hard work and sweat to get where they are. Their work was unknown, unseen, and unnoticed possibly for year after year, but they still did it. They had the discipline, the drive, the belief. They chose to do it. They paid their dues to get to the top. That's what it takes: Sacrifice. Commitment. Hard work.

Remember that and ask yourself, "Am I willing to pay the price for what I want to achieve?" Are you willing to make that choice? Are you willing to sacrifice? We must all count the cost. Anything that is worthwhile in life takes time, sweat, and determination.

In my situation, I knew that I would have to continually battle to put my life back together. I also knew that I would have to fight through these things all the way until I reached a point of final decision and had triumphed and overcome them so that I could get on with my life.

Since I was a child, I've always had a fierce competitive nature. This same fierce *will-to-win* and *never-give-up* attitude now helped me in my struggle against despair and anguish over the loss of so much in my life.

I had a basis for the faith in myself to never give up. During my freshman year in high school, I had fought to make the junior varsity baseball team. Here I was—Rico Petrocelli's nephew—supposed to be a great player because of my uncle's reputation, not mine, and I was fighting to make the team. The first half of the season, I ended up not starting, but I worked hard to prove myself and ended up starting the second half of the season.

The highlight of the year was when I hit a grand slam against one of the top teams in our district. I finished up strong and ended up as one of the best players on the team. The main point here was that I never gave up. I remembered that, even if you start slowly, you can finish strong—and that will make a difference.

My sophomore year in high school, the JV baseball program was cut for budget reasons. I tried out for the varsity, but partly due to an injury, I didn't make the team. I said to myself that I was going to work harder and make the team as a junior. That summer I worked harder and harder, and made the varsity team. In both my junior and senior years, I started in centerfield and made a name for myself in baseball.

When I attended ORU, I tried out for the team my first two years. After not making the varsity either time, I vowed over the summer between my sophomore and junior years that I would work harder than ever and come back and make the team. That summer I lifted weights, I ran, I took batting practice, and worked hard. I was ready for tryouts that fall. After the first day of tryouts, the coach came up to me and said, "I can't believe how much you've improved." I was determined. I worked hard to develop the skills that

God gave me. My reward was that I ended up making the team both my junior and senior years at ORU. We were ranked number one in the NCAA Division I for most of the 1981 season.

Fear had invaded my heart and was trying to destroy me in any way it could. Anytime I went to sleep, in the back of my mind I wasn't sure that I wouldn't once again wake up in the same nightmare situation. Day in and day out I had to fight the battle against fear constantly. I wondered if I would ever have a full life again or if I would ever teach again. Could I ever love again? Would people laugh at me or accept the way I looked? They were legitimate questions.

Could I go to sleep at night in peace and not fear someone else crashing into my house? That may seem crazy to have a fear of that, but can you imagine anyone ever believing that such a thing could happen in the first place? Fear can cloud your mind and your heart so that you can't enjoy things fully. After a traumatic event, fear is always lurking in the back of your mind.

The strongest battle I fought was overcoming guilt. How could I enjoy life again? Ava was dead. How could I ever laugh again? Ava was dead. How could I ever look for love again? Ava was my love. I felt that I was now turning my back on her. Why didn't I lift the truck off of her? Why didn't I dig her out? Why didn't I get to her? If she was my wife, why didn't I protect her? It's my fault she died. It happened because I'm no good. If I didn't make the mistakes I made, then she would be alive.

Guilt feeds on fear, judgment, and condemnation. I felt guilty that just two weeks before the accident we had switched the sides of the bed that we slept on. What if we had not switched, and I had been on the other side? Maybe I could have withstood the impact. We had also talked about sleeping in a different bedroom. What if we had slept in another room? Maybe she wouldn't be dead. What if we had rented one of the other houses farther back? What if I had taken that job up in New Jersey? We wouldn't have been in Texas at all. I had to live with the guilt of all of these questions. "What if" and "I should have" controlled my mind. Why didn't I die? Why was she taken and I wasn't?

While I lived with Ava's family following the accident, I sometimes wondered what they were thinking. Did they ask, "Why did Ava have to die?

Why wasn't it Bobby?" I don't know if they ever thought that, but I couldn't help but realize how difficult it must have been for them.

Even in the hospital immediately following the accident—it had only been hours since Ava's death—I sat there on the gurney in the hallway and wondered if Ava's family wished it had been me who had been killed instead of her. Fear brings bondage. I have heard an acronym for fear: False Evidence Appearing Real. We need to learn from President Franklin Delano Roosevelt who said those famous words in the time of crisis, "The only thing to fear is fear itself."

Ava's Uncle Ted was a bright star to me early in my dealing with the tragedy. Uncle Ted came one day to visit me in the hospital. This particular day, guilt was ruling my mind. Maybe Uncle Ted sensed something. He leaned over my bed and whispered in my ear, "Bobby, I want you to know that we're all so glad you're alive. We're not happy that Ava was killed, but we are happy that *you're* alive. We love you—because you're family, too." Those words spoke life to me. It confirmed the power of our words to bring life or death, hope or despair.

Life is filled with battles. We all fight against fear, guilt, confusion, pain, bitterness, hatred, rejection, and even unforgiveness. We must press on and not allow obstacles to hinder our progress. A true champion may lose a battle, but the fight in him is so fierce that he picks himself up to fight on and win the war. Increase your perceived value. This is how you see yourself. It's what you think you are worth. It's time to increase it. Remember, you are the only person in history that has been created for your life's assignment. Live it to the fullest. *You* are the only one who can stop you from achieving it. Don't be your own worst enemy.

CHAPTER

17

Hope Is a Good Thing

H ope is a good thing, maybe even the best of things, and good things never die," is a phrase that is often used in one of my favorite movies, *Shawshank Redemption*. People are in desperate search of whatever and whomever will bring them hope. People need to be on a diet of hope. When we think about "feeding," we automatically think about food, or at least I do. Well, I had to not only feed my body, but also other areas of my life that needed special nourishment. I had to choose to feed my mind, my body, and my spirit good things. "You are what you eat." It's true. And this applies to all areas of your life—not just the physical part.

While attending Oral Roberts University, the importance of feeding and uplifting every part of your life, "the whole man," was heavily emphasized. Learning to live a balanced life was one thing that was always stressed. Build your spirit, body, and mind. As you do this you not only strengthen your faith and love, but also hope. When people have hope they feel invincible. I knew that it was tremendously important that I have all three of these areas in some sort of balance in my life to achieve victory. I ran to whatever brought it to me.

One area that transcends all ages, faiths, cultures, and ethnic groups is music. People love music. It seems to be one of the common bonds of the human race. We were all created to enjoy some form of music. We don't have to like the same style or rhythm, but give us music. I believe that there are two kinds of music—that which exhorts (lifts up) and that which tears down. The goal is to find your style with an affirmative message that will enhance all parts of your life—music that brings hope and help to a world in pain. Music truly affects a person's attitude and mood. Positive music feeds your mind good, healthy, and wholesome things. Negative music can tear down your spirit and have a detrimental effect on you as a person. I had to make sure that I was listening to positive music. Music is such a huge part of my life. I listen to music when I wake up in the morning. I listen to music on the drive to work every day. Sometimes at work, I may be able to softly play some background music. It was imperative that I listen to music that would build me up and not tear me down. I personally enjoy many different types, styles, and forms. I guess I am eclectic in my taste.

I'm a big fan of praise and worship music. This is positive music—music that renews and refreshes your mind and spirit. It's uplifting and has the power of restoration. I believe there is power in praise. I listened to praise music to help lift my spirit when I felt despair. Happy, upbeat music put me in a good frame of mind. When your spirit is uplifted, the rest of your being feels invigorated; therefore, you facilitate a greater sense of hope.

Another road to hope was listening to dynamic speakers, preachers, teachers, and motivators. Who would have thought that this would eventually prepare me to take hope to others as a speaker? I love people that realize the importance of helping others. People like Tom Landry, former coach of the Dallas Cowboys; John Wooden, the legendary basketball coach of UCLA; Norman Vincent Peale, author of *The Power of Positive Thinking*; Robert Schuller, from the Crystal Cathedral in California; Oral Roberts, who always said, "God is my source"; Don Shula, the inspirational legendary head coach of the Miami Dolphins; and probably my favorite of all, Tony Campolo (who would eventually help President Clinton during his turbulent times). Presently Oprah Winfrey, Dr. Phil, and Tony Robbins are among my favorites. What makes them all so desirable to listen to is the fact that they bring hope to all in a real way. People flock to those who are real and genuine. This is why I am so surprised that many people of faith would use so much fear, guilt, judgment, control, manipulation, and condemnation to attract others. As the expression goes, "You attract more bees with honey." It's the goodness of God that draws people to Him.

This daily regimen of feeding my mind positive poems, letters, books, and magazines encouraged me to persevere and press on, and to never, ever give up. I had a steady "diet" of uplifting music and positive speakers to consume. Sometimes I needed an appetizer, other times a soup or salad and, occasionally, a full-course dinner, depending on how I felt at that moment. The best thing about feeding on positive morsels like this was that I could never be guilty of overeating. I could "eat" to my heart's content. I needed the nourishment and realized that I had to constantly renew my mind, my body, and my spirit. The psychological trauma had wounded my spirit so deeply that I needed to rejuvenate it with good things.

In addition to getting my mind back in good shape, I also began to get back into shape physically. I began to train on weights again, lifting every other day, doing lat pulls, bent-over rows, tricep extensions, squats, and bench presses.

I also began light jogging and jogging in the pool to increase my endurance and aerobic capacity. I was expending more energy during the day and therefore had to refuel more often. I had to make sure that I fed my body good food—like fruits, vegetables, and other healthy items—and not junk foods that would stunt my growth and hinder my progress. Being from a physical education background, I knew that exercise and diet go hand in hand when it comes to athletic performance. Since I realized I could've easily been more seriously injured, I was excited that I could still work out, play basketball, and exercise.

As I physically got stronger and back into shape, I also felt much more confident about my appearance. For the longest time, I had reservations about going to the beach—one of my favorite places in all the world. But because of the scars and blemishes that will never go away, I had to accept the fact that every time I wore shorts and a short-sleeved shirt, people knowingly and unknowingly would stare at me. I had to get used to small children pointing and cringing at the sight of the deep, massive scars on my legs and arms.

"Mommy, mommy. Look at that man's arm!" a little girl would innocently yell so that the whole beach could hear.

"Honey, it's not polite to... Oh, my gosh—George. George. What do you think happened to that man over there? Jessica, stop pointing."

Believe me, I've heard it all. Sometimes, if someone asked me what happened, I'd be tempted to say with a straight face, "Oh, I was swimming in three or four feet of water right out there and a great white shark bit me about this same time last year. A lot of people think they're deadly, but I survived okay, see?" I never did, though. That would've been really mean. I just took a deep breath, gained my composure, and explained to them the story. Most of them were apologetic and receptive after that. People do need to think before speaking. I am still learning that everyday.

Spiritually, I prayed, attended church, listened to praise music, read the Bible, and referred to other self-help inspirational books. Please know that during times when I was spiritually frustrated, it didn't change God's love for me or my faith in Him. Being angry at God at times will never change who He is or His love for you. Mentally, my mind was being renewed by meditating and thinking upon good things: Wholesome music, inspirational leaders, uplifting poems, positive writings, and motivating speakers. Physically, I balanced my diet with exercise. Focusing on all three areas was the only way for me to gain a total victory and get my life back together.

Another way that I was able to cope with the grief from the tragedy was to fill my heart with laughter—joyous, hearty laughter. "A merry heart doeth good like a medicine" (Proverbs 17:22). Since I am a huge fan of many of the classic television comedies, one of my favorite escapes was to watch various episodes of my favorites. This was wonderful therapy for me because if I were feeling sad or depressed, I could pop in some tapes and sit there for hours and laugh hysterically at the antics on *F-Troop*, *I Love Lucy*, *Gilligan's Island*, *The Three Stooges*, *The Honeymooners*, and the *Munsters*. One moment I was sobbing tears of pain, in the next moment I was laughing tears of joy. Even today some of my favorite times are watching the reruns of *Seinfeld*. You can never get too much laughter.

One of my favorite *Three Stooges* episodes is when Curly dressed up like a gorilla. One of my favorite *Lucy* shows is "Vitameatavegamin," where she was the spokeswoman for a new health supplement. A favorite *Honeymooners* episode is when Norton was teaching Ralph to dance, another to play golf. The chemistry between Art Carney and Jackie Gleason on that show helped to make it one of the best of all time. And one of the most memorable *Little Rascals* short films is the one in which Alfalfa fights for Darla's affection by building a boat to race Waldo, the rich snobby kid. I love that particular one because it has Spanky, Buckwheat, and Porky in it also.

After all these years, I have an extensive collection of these nostalgic and classic comedies. Every once in a while, when I need a good strong, belly laugh, I'll pop in a tape and away I'll go. There's a lot of truth to the statement, "Garbage in; garbage out." I like to say, "Positive in; positive out."

Remember that the sum total of what you are as a person is only as good as the sum total of the parts that you put in. We are who we are today because of all the decisions we have made. Our past defines our present, and how we react to our past, defines our future.

CHAPTER 18

Can I Love Again?

When school ended in the spring of 1986, I knew that Texas was not where I wanted to stay. I had enjoyed many wonderful times, but the pain and memory of losing Ava at times was overwhelming. I returned to New York to find myself again, and to determine which direction I wanted to go with my life. I thought I would feel more comfortable in familiar surroundings so back to New York I went. I didn't know what was ahead for me—but I felt a peace about taking the step.

Mineola High School on Long Island hired me as a full-time substitute teacher and junior varsity and varsity football coach for the first two months of the fall semester. Though I had just spent three years as a full-time teacher and coach in Texas, I knew that here I was starting over. I also knew this was the first step to securing a full-time teaching position.

Fortunately, I didn't have to wait long. In the short time that I was in Mineola, I gained a lot of favor with the faculty, students, and staff. I also found a new strength in myself that would eventually point me in the direction of becoming a full-time motivational speaker.

Mineola High School had one of the best Students Against Driving Drunk (SADD) programs in the country. It is now called Students Against Destructive Decisions. The sponsor and student leaders of the group asked me to share my story in their major fall assembly program. Representatives from *Reader's Digest* magazine, politicians, and many successful community leaders were to be in attendance. The audience was predicted to be around one thousand people. The date of the assembly would be October 25, 1986, exactly one year to the day after the accident. I was nervous to be speaking so soon after the accident.

For weeks prior to the program, I wrote down ideas and prepared for what I would speak about that day. I not only wanted to give a good speech, but I also wanted to communicate as sincerely as possible that no one should *ever* have to go through what I had gone through. The loss was too great, and the pain was too deep. I wanted to strongly and effectively relay the message that had to be driven home—that this type of tragedy *could have* been and *can* be prevented in the future. I didn't sleep well the night before the program. I was too excited and nervous, hoping that it would go well and that the response would be positive.

"The reason that I'm standing before you today... " I had practiced my speech a hundred times before actually standing in front of this audience, going over and over the key points, and stressing different parts of it to get the proper emphasis. I was so pumped up; I bet everybody thought I was going to explode. You see, I'm the type of person who tells it like it is—what you see is what you get. I would never be good in poker because I wear my heart on my sleeve and my emotions show in my face too easily. I'm a straightforward kind of guy, and I don't beat around the bush. Maybe that's my strongest point in speaking—that I come across as genuine and sincere.

I want so badly to communicate effectively that I just bluntly tell the truth.

The day of the speech was a landmark day for me, the beginning of a new era in my life. After the first few moments of my speech, something kicked in. I think it was the fact that I was just telling my story, with no sugarcoating whatsoever. The truth and reality came through to the audience that day, and their response was exhilarating. I knew in my heart that from my speaking for the very first time in that assembly program at Mineola High School on October 25, 1986, seeds were planted for my future in speaking and helping young people with my message. This was the first time that I began to see that somehow God was going to bring good out of something that was terrible—a miracle that only He could do.

Since things had gone so well in my short time at Mineola High School, by November I was offered a full-time teaching position in the East Norwich-Oyster Bay School District. I was now teaching physical education and was a high school assistant coach in football, baseball, and basketball. This was only the beginning of more good things to come. I was happy to be back in familiar territory. Long Island is a lot different than the Brooklyn area, but, hey, it's New York. Family is very close by. I felt a peace about the move from Texas, and landing the teaching position after only a few months was confirmation that I had made the right choice.

It was now a year and a half since the accident and I was starting to feel better about myself in more areas of my life. I was teaching and coaching in a new environment. I was spending time with the kids whom I loved, and I was in familiar and comfortable surroundings. I was now thinking about the possibility of companionship. I was open to a relationship, but decided that I would not actively seek one out. A lot of people were giving me different advice about that area of my life. One would say, "Go to this club and find a nice girl. There are tons of beautiful girls there. So-and-so met a girl there, and they've been going out for three months now. Who knows? They might even get married. They're talking about living together first. You ever thought about trying that for awhile?"

Someone else would say, "Bobby, come on. You're young. Just go out and pick one. There are all kinds of fish in the sea. Just throw out your hook and reel one in." Another would say, "I've got a friend who has a sister in her mid-twenties. She doesn't go out much, but she's a very nice girl. She's smart, intelligent, has a lot of brains—a really sharp girl. Did I mention that she's very nice? Her mother keeps telling her, 'Live a little. Take off three of those sweaters, shave, and go out on a date like a good girl…'" Everybody tried to give me advice about love. I was beginning to think that maybe I was ready for a relationship, but I wanted it to come naturally.

It wasn't long until I met a beautiful young woman by the name of Suzanne Marie Nick. She was from Long Island, and she was absolutely gorgeous. She was from a strong family with a traditional Catholic background. Her ethnic heritage was Polish and German. I remember the first time I laid eyes on her. A coaching friend had introduced her to me while we were getting pizza at a small pizzeria on Long Island. When I said "Hi" to her, my heart almost leaped out of my throat. "My name is Bobby Petrocelli… It's nice to meet you," I said as my jaw dropped to the floor. She was a Babe—with a capital B.

Babe-a-lonia. Babe-a-licious. Babe-raham Lincoln. She could've said, "Fourscore and seven years ago…" and I would've hung on every word. I think she felt the same about me because when our eyes met, we both experienced a deep, fixating gaze, as if we were both spellbound and entranced with each other. I'll never forget that feeling. It was a moment of unmistakable connection—like two puzzle pieces finding their matching groove. The fit was there. We knew something exciting would be happening for as long as we wanted it to. But the best part about it was that we knew from that first moment there was something special between us.

Everybody called her Suzy. I liked that. Even her name had a ring to it. Suzy Nick. I've been told that one of the major differences between men and women is that men are much more stimulated by sight, and women are more stimulated by how they're treated. Well, whatever the case, Suzy had caught my eye. She was a knockout. She had long, athletic legs with well-defined calves. She had the face of a beautiful fashion model. Her hair was long and dark, the kind she could fix in a million different ways so the style would always look fresh and new. Her personality was full of energy, full of life, and a lot of fun to be with. She had everything that I liked in a woman—in abundance, I might add. She was a fifteen-plus on a scale of one to ten. And, to top it off, she was an athlete, a volleyball and basketball player. Without question, she had an *invisible touch*. I remember that first time I met Suzy. She looked at me in such a way. *Wow!* I said to myself. There was a gleam in her eyes, and my eyes were gleaming, too, and my smile was beaming.

Suzy was young and full of life. She caused my heart to skip a beat. Before this time I had felt a void—a place that only a special woman could fill. Now I hoped and prayed Suzy would be that special woman. Something was definitely there—something magical between us. Some people look for this kind of magic all of their lives. I was ecstatic to think that I'd found it—again. Is it true? Am I being blessed for the second time in my life?

As Suzy and I grew closer in our relationship, I was still haunted by doubts that I could ever really love again. Could I? I wasn't sure. I did know that she brought much joy into my life when I was with her—the kind of joy that I had longed for—a joy that I had known God would restore.

With every girlfriend in my life, I've always looked for the chemistry between us. There's a lot to be said about how you feel when you're around a person. Does she make you feel comfortable? Are you able to be yourself in any situation? Does she make you a better person? Are you making her a better person? This is what I call chemistry. There's got to be that special kind of bonding, like two halves fitting together to make a whole.

I felt this with Suzy. We liked a lot of the same things. She liked different ethnic foods. She liked Italian dishes. Our first date was at an Italian restaurant in Brooklyn named Callaro's. I can still remember what Suzy ordered: chicken parmesan—great! It is one of my favorite dishes, also. I remember how nervous we both were as we ate our food, wanting to make the proper impression. We continually enjoyed Italian food especially after I rediscovered Spumoni Gardens. I grew up going there but hadn't been back in years. It truly became our favorite with their mouth-watering center-cut Sicilian pizza—better known as 'squares.'

At first, Suzy wasn't thrilled with another favorite food of mine—Mexican. Spending four years in Texas, I fell in love with Mexican food. But after I introduced her to Chi Chi's and then, authentic Mexican food, she quickly became accustomed to it, and today Mexican is one of her favorite foods. She now craves Mexican foods—Hallelujah!

She loved sports and also loved to *watch* sports with me. She didn't mind watching college football or basketball with me—which are two of my favorite sports to watch. I love college sports, maybe even more than the pros.

We even shared the same idiosyncrasies. I'm an ex-baseball player and she's an ex-softball player, and occasionally we talked about our habits while playing. "You're probably going to think this is weird…" I started to say, and then changed my mind. "Well… never mind." "You can't start a statement like that and not finish it," she scolded me.

"Well, it's kind of a silly thing and you probably won't understand. When I play sports…"

"…you can't chew gum and play at the same time," she interjected before I could finish.

"That's right. How'd you know that?" I asked.

"You can't do it because it ruins your concentration," she continued.

"Right. I can't. Who told you that?"

"I just knew," Suzy said. "I can't chew gum and play sports at the same time either. It ruins my concentration."

I couldn't believe it. This to me was a major connection. How did she know I felt that way? And how in the world did I meet somebody I liked so well and who, on top of everything, had exactly the same weird problem in playing sports. To me, this was nothing short of miraculous. It *had* to be God who had brought us together. Things just don't happen this way.

I quickly realized that *this* woman was special. We really clicked. Certain things truly impressed me about Suzy. I was eight years older than her, but she had a great maturity about her. Could I really be falling madly in love with a younger woman?

I was impressed and touched by her interest in me as a person. She asked questions about my life—my relationship with Ava—and talked about how hard it must have been to work through the tragedy. She seemed to have a genuine love, concern, and compassion for me. She was genuinely interested in what made me tick. She expressed herself in such a way that it made me feel whole again—comfortable and attractive again. When I looked at Suzy, I could see that she had strong feelings towards me, too. I could see it simply and truthfully in her eyes—she really loved me. I knew it was more than a physical thing because just to be with her was special in itself. I knew that love had bitten me again—and once again it left deep tooth marks. She complimented me. She knew when to think before speaking—something I still struggle with at times.

The first gift Suzy ever gave me was at the beach. We were on our second date when she handed me a gift-wrapped box. "I have something for you, Bobby," she said as we sat on the edge of the pier. I took the box and felt that it had definite weight to it. I smiled at her, not knowing what to say because she had caught me off guard and taken me by surprise. But I loved every minute of it. I slowly peeled away the gift wrapping and opened the box. My eyes lit up as I saw what the contents were—a spray bottle of Obsession cologne. Was she trying to tell me something? Whatever it was, I didn't care. All I know is the next time she saw me I was wearing Obsession. If Suzy gave it to me because it was her favorite, I would wear it every minute of every day.

Looking back at it now, that's one of the reasons that I liked to be with her. It was because she often surprised me with things like this. She was often unpredictable—so full of life, energy, and unpredictability. But the best thing was, she enjoyed being that way just for me.

The more time I spent with her, the more I fell in love with Suzy. We would talk for hours, whether at the beach, on the phone, or just sitting around the house. I felt so comfortable with her—she was so very easy to open up to. I liked that she asked questions and really wanted to know the answers. I liked that she wasn't the type of woman who only wanted to talk about herself and her own problems. I liked that she wasn't the type of woman to take and not give back.

She never seemed to be threatened that I had been married before—that impressed me to no end. She accepted it as part of my life. She realized that she couldn't change the past, but that maybe she could become part of my future. She loved me for who I was. I began to ask myself, "Could I love twice? Could I be so privileged to meet such an incredible woman?" My hopes ran high. Why shouldn't they? We had so much in common and had hit it off so well. There had to be a future for us somewhere. This relationship was feeling too comfortable and too complete for it not to lead to more. I just knew something extra special was there.

One night at my mother's house in Brooklyn, I knew Suzy had to pass the biggest test of all. I popped in a *Three Stooges* video to see her response. If she laughed, then she wasn't the girl for me. But if she laughed *hysterically*—I was on the right track. Suzy fell on the floor laughing so hard it brought tears to her eyes. My eyes also began to tear, not necessarily because of the Stooges antics, but because I now realized that love had truly found me again.

Perhaps the icing on the cake was that Suzy had a great desire to know more about God. This, to me, was encouraging and important. I saw the depth that she had in her life, and it electrified me. She understood the importance of the greater things in life.

One evening when I went back home after dropping Suzy at her place, I sat in my house and wondered if this was really happening. *Please let this love be real*, I said to God. For the longest time I had thought that there was some sort of curse on me that would keep me from ever being in love again. Isn't that something? What a lie. What an outright lie! But the sad thing is, there are people today who are feeling this way. They think that there is some kind of curse that is keeping them from some type of happiness. There is not. Let me say it again—*there is not*. That's a lie—a lie that has to be dealt with. We have to increase our perceived value or self worth. Still I was afraid that if I invested my love in Suzy that maybe, just maybe, the same thing would happen, and she too would be taken from me. Can you see the kind of fear that I was still living under? When bad things happen to us, many times we tend to shut down. We withdraw out of fear. We have to choose not to do this, but Suzy helped put to rest some of these fears.

On what would have been my fourth wedding anniversary if Ava were still alive—March 12, 1987—I was at Suzy's house when she handed me several big bags of presents. They were brand new clothes from the Gap. You're never too old to fall into the Gap.

I didn't know why I was being blessed this way.

"You know why!" she exclaimed.

I pondered, confused.

"You know what day this is, don't you?" she asked. I wasn't sure what she was talking about. Then it dawned on me. She was so concerned about what type of negative emotions I might have that day that she wanted to do something positive for me to cheer me up. She thought I would be upset since it would have been my fourth wedding anniversary with Ava. Now, I knew more than ever that I wanted a serious relationship with her. She could have been fearful, jealous, and insecure. She laid down those feelings because she felt what I could be going through was more important. She realized for this moment, it wasn't about her and her feelings. My involvement with Suzy was now allowing me to put my past in the proper perspective. Suzy knew how much I enjoyed writing my thoughts and feelings down in a journal and had bought one for me. In March 1987 I wrote this down after she gave it to me:

My life has been through so much. I thank You, Lord, for always seeing me through. You have always been there for me. You have now given me the chance to love again, such a wonderful, loving, and understanding young lady to share my life with. The last several months have only been the beginning of many more wonderful months and years in our relationship. Let us always keep our hearts and eyes focused on You.

It's through Your loving hand that we can experience the love we have for each other. Help us to encourage, build up, and not tear down one another. Jesus, let your peace and love guide us through all the journeys of our lives together. Give me the strength to overcome fear, doubt, and insecurity. Let Your confidence rule in my life, for You are my confidence and strength.

Thank You again for Suzy, Your precious gift to me. Let me be precious to her always. Guide us to lead others to Your saving and loving grace. Help us to be strong in You. To please You, our God, in all we do.

"Hey, why don't we ride to the beach today?" I nonchalantly asked Suzy on June 2, 1988, when I met her after work. "We can go to Angelo's Pizza and get a bite to eat. How's that sound?" I had just come from Donato's Jewelry Store in the heart of the "Diamond Exchange" in Manhattan.

"Fine," Suzy said, unwittingly.

It was a sunny day and we arrived at the Jones Beach West End-2 at 4:30. The beach was virtually empty, so we walked and talked and casually strolled around the sand. A couple of times I thought the timing was right, but I didn't do it. Then, about five o'clock, after we had been talking for a while, I dropped to both knees.

"Suzy, what are you doing for the next fifty years?" I asked. "I was wondering if you wouldn't mind marrying me very much?"

She waved her arms in the air like a chicken trying desperately to fly and started screaming, "Yes! Yes! Yes! I will! I will! I *will* marry you!"

She cried, laughed, and jumped around like a jumping bean. The sea gulls ran for cover and the ocean did "the wave." When she said "Yes," it brought such joy to my heart. All those times of doubt and despair had been shattered. God had blessed me with two diamonds—a 1.12 carat marquise ring from Donato's and, more importantly, a precious diamond of a woman, in Suzanne Marie Nick. We saved two special shells from the beach that day, to remind us of that wonderful day when Suzy said "Yes" and jumped around like a jumping bean.

On May 6, 1989, Suzy and I were married in a beautiful garden ceremony at Westbury Manor in Westbury, New York. To give you another example of God's blessings on me, rain had fallen for several straight days before the ceremony, and we were disappointed early that Saturday morning because it looked as if we would have to hold the wedding indoors. But wouldn't you know, about forty-five minutes before the ceremony, the skies cleared and we were able to be married outside. It had rained for days and days and days, and this was the first time it had cleared up. Is God faithful? I know that He was smiling a big smile on that day.

It was awesome to have the family and friends who had supported me through my trials and the tragedy now be part of this victorious celebration. I think they were almost as happy for me as I was. I said *almost*. The wedding was such a joy-filled celebration. Everything about it was special. You could feel it.

The reception dinner was terrific, also. Since Suzy had never been married before and we were starting our life together, I tried to make it as special as possible. I sang to her a ballad called, "I've Waited a Lifetime." Right after my best man Jay Ferraro proposed a toast, I asked for the microphone, sat Suzy in the middle of the room in a chair, and started to sing with an accompaniment tape.

"I've waited a lifetime
To stand here looking in your eyes.
Now it's finally coming true.
With the Lord as my witness,
I'll love you for the rest of my days,
Don't you ever go away.
Nobody else
Can make me smile the way you do.
Nobody else
Can ever win my heart like you... "

Suzy cried, and I saw everyone in the place crying—family, friends, guests, waiters, waitresses, the maitre d'—even the band. It was an emotional and special time for not only me, but for everyone who loved both Suzy and me. There was barely a dry eye in the house. Cheeks told me it was because my voice was so terrible. He said I broke two mirrors, three priceless crystal sculptures, and Mrs. O'Leary's glasses. You see the kind of friends I have? You see the kind of abuse I take?

I know they were crying because they realized all that I had gone through. This was the day I got a second chance at love. My family and friends knew the pain and devastation I had been through, and now to see me with such joy in my heart filled their eyes with tears. Person after person came up to us after the ceremony and said that it was one of the best times that they had ever had at a wedding. There was such an overwhelming sense of celebration and sheer joy, that it enveloped the room with its warmth and blanketed us all with a true feeling of happiness. I was starting over, but it was a new beginning for my princess, my beautiful baby, Suzy. Following the celebration and reception, Suzy and I spent our wedding night at the La Guardia Airport Marriott. I spent a major part of the evening crying tears of joy. For the first three hours of my honeymoon I held her in my arms thanking her for giving me a second chance at love and life.

We walked into the room and nearly fell over with exhaustion. That's when it hit us. I think it hit me first, and then Suzy's reaction to my tearful release was to also cry. It felt so cleansing to get it out. All my emotion from the past several years was released when I allowed myself to weep tears of joy. My life had almost been destroyed, but was now looking full of hope and promise. That to me was nothing short of a miracle. We were both so thankful to God for bringing us together.

Suzy and I honeymooned in the Outer Banks of North Carolina. We were planning a longer honeymoon cruise later that summer because I couldn't afford much time off from work in May.

We had moved to Virginia in August 1988 and I was teaching physical education and coaching football at Great Bridge High School in Chesapeake. Suzy was a student at Old Dominion University in Norfolk, completing her degree.

Following our honeymoon, we returned to Chesapeake where we had purchased a new home. The cost of living in Virginia was much less than in New York, and we were able to have a beautiful, traditional brick home built for much less than in New York. Our new home had hardwood floors, a fireplace, cherry furniture, four bedrooms, lots of space, and a beautiful yard, and was in a new development.

I stood in the bedroom of our new home and said to Suzy, "The last four years I've felt like a nomad, a wanderer, a man who couldn't call any place 'home.' Now that we're married and together, I want you to know that I feel I *am* home again." I tried to hold it back, but the emotion was too strong to suppress any longer. I felt a freedom in my heart as I began to cry—the joy of starting our lives together had overwhelmed me. I couldn't keep it inside.

Suzy held me as I cried for several minutes. "I love you, Bobby Petrocelli. There's nothing in this world that can keep you from my love. Always remember that," she sweetly whispered in my ear as she embraced me tighter. I hugged her back, but there was no way I could've gotten close enough to her at that moment. We had become one, and I had become whole again. Suzy and I try to live life to the fullest. To this day we enjoy traveling, cruising, hanging out on the beach, spending time with family and friends. I realize more then ever she is my best friend. I love doing things with my best friend and want for her to experience the best in life. Knowing she takes me for better and worse means the world. Maybe it's time to start a family.

"No man can possibly know what life means, what the world means, until he has a child and loves it. And then the whole universe changes and nothing will ever again seem exactly as it seemed before."—this was a quote I read by Lafcadio Hearn.

One fear that kept creeping up and showing its ugly face through those years after the tragedy was that I wasn't sure I could father children. When the truck ran over me, my testicles were injured, and they swelled up to the size of a tennis ball. I was too embarrassed about it to have a doctor check to see if I was sterile, but in the back of my mind I constantly wondered if I would ever have children. I love kids and wanted the chance to have a family and be a father, but I didn't know if I could. Then it happened.

On April 11, 1992, at 3:30 p.m., that fear was put to rest, when my first child, my first son Alec Robert Petrocelli was born. It was a miracle. I never thought that such a little red person could bring me such joy. Cheeks called him the "Red Man of Courage." Alec Robert. If it were up to Suzy, his name would have been Alec Tom Cruise Petrocelli. You see what type of wife I have? My first child was eight pounds, twelve ounces, and twenty-one inches long—a future defensive lineman. The Giants need him bad. He is adorable, so beautiful and handsome, and looks just like his daddy.

Rarely as a child did I call him Alec. I called him Pookey Hahny. What silly names we call our children. "What's up, Champ? What are you looking at, Pookey Hahny? Are you looking at Daddy?" I say to him in his crib. It's silly, isn't it, the way we talk to babies, probably because they bring us so much happiness. And we can't believe that a human life started from a little seed. How can people say there are no miracles happening today? How can people say, "There is no God?" Every time a child is born it's both a miracle *and* a beautiful gift from God.

Suzy spent six hours in labor after her water broke. Alec had a large head and it took more time to push him out than normal. He got stuck twice, once in the cervix and once in the birth canal. Finally, a vacuum extractor was brought in to help bring Alec into the world. Suzy was a tough cookie. She had Alec by natural childbirth. No epidural—no sedation—she used nothing. She said to me later that the pain was excruciating, but she didn't want any chemical helpers to slow down the process. Fortunately for her, she has a high threshold for pain.

I stayed with Suzy the whole time, never showing a trace of anxiety. Finally, when Alec was born, I walked out in the hall and wept uncontrollably. I was not only touched that Alec was born, but that Suzy was okay, too. I probably looked worse than Suzy after Alec was born. (Cheeks said I looked like Herman Munster. You see what kind of friends I have?)

My sister and cousins were at the hospital. Their fondest memory of Alec's birth was when I came out to tell them. Instead of telling them if it was a boy or a girl, I just told them that the baby's head was as big as a hospital. "You should have seen the size of his head! It was humongous! I've never seen a baby's head that big before."

"Well, I guess he had a boy then," said my sister Chrissy. "So, you're going to name him Bighead, huh? Or maybe Hugh—short for Humongo? Or better yet—Mel—short for Melon—because he's got a huge one?"

Four years later it happened again. On June 2, 1996, my second son, Aron James Petrocelli was born. I have been blessed again. Before Aron was born, the doctors were concerned because he had an accelerated heart rate. Suzy had to be put on medication. When he was born, hallelujah, there was no trace of the problem. I called him Mister Mister. Suzy was happy to call him A.J.

I feel as if I've had everything doubly restored to me. Everything had been taken from me: my wife, my home, my health, and my future. Then, years later, it was restored back. I have a great wife, a new home, my health, a future, and our newest joys, my sons Alec Robert and Aron James, better known as Pookey Hahny and Mister Mister.

Every time I look at Suzy and them, I'm so grateful that I never gave up until I found such a wonderful woman. Otherwise, I would have never seen Alec and Aron's births. I would never have gotten to hear them say "Da Da" for the first time—something they said way before they said "momma." I would've missed out on the experience of being in a Cracker Barrel restaurant when Alec was one year old and seeing him make a rooster hairdo with the mashed potatoes, put peas up his nose and corn in his ears, and have chicken hanging on his face. The entire ten-foot area in every direction around his high chair looked like a battle zone. I would have missed picking him up from the high chair and walking him out the door with food dropping from inside his pants with every step he took. I would have missed Aron telling me in the car to stop talking to mommy. "Why?" I asked.

"I am trying to talk to myself and I can't hear what I am saying."

I remember when Alec was younger I was relaxing at home, sitting around in sweats and a T-shirt. Alec came up to me and innocently looked at the large prominent scar on my arm. He stared at it for a few seconds, pointed his little finger, and said, "Boo-boo." I smiled at him with tears streaming down my face and nodded, "Yes." He looked up at me with his amazing eyes, then I grabbed him and hugged him as if I had never hugged him before. Since Aron has been young, I always say, "Aron, can I ask you a question?" His response is, "I know, Daddy, how come I love you so much?" It's awesome to watch both Alec and Aron while they sleep. I also love to pray over them—to cover them with blankets. They bring so much joy to our hearts. They never become too old to be called my little boys.

Alec and Aron are daddy's champs. They are my miracle boys. Maybe someday they'll understand. They and Suzy have brought such joy and love back into my life after my not having any for such a long time. That's something I'll make sure they always understand.

"The thief cometh not, but for to steal, and to kill, and to destroy. I am come that they might have life, and that they might have it more abundantly" (John 10:10).

It's Always Something—
Par for the Course

L ife is continually filled with obstacles, with adversity, with loss, with pain, and with rejection. But at the same time, it's also filled with faith, with hope, with peace, with joy, and with love. Our response to what happens to us in our lives is the key. It's the essential element. As I mentioned earlier, in life we can be sure, there will be pain. How we respond to that pain affects not only us, but the lives of others. You never know what someone could be going through. People respond out of pain, both good and bad. The key is learning how to respond in a positive manner.

Several years ago I got a letter from a man name John. He had gotten a copy of my book, *Triumph over Tragedy*. He was happy to see I had been moving forward. Then he shared his story. John and his wife had both been paramedics at the scene who had tried desperately to save Ava's life. I began crying as I felt his pain. Then the tears really flowed when John shared further that his wife had been so distraught that she couldn't save Ava, and this, plus the pain of other tragedies, was more than she could handle—and she eventually committed suicide. My heart broke for John.

An important principle that we must take to heart is what I call the Ten-Second Principle. Our lives are built on ten-second decisions. Foundations are built on or destroyed by ten-second decisions. Think about how important a simple "Yes" or "No" can be in a situation. It's vital to learn to make good choices and to put them into practice. The key is in learning how to make good ten-second choices so that, when turmoil or difficulties arise, your foundation will be strong and you will win out in the end.

Life is not fair—it will never be fair. Think about it. Is it easier to do what is right or what is wrong? Let's be honest. It's much easier to do what's wrong. We all struggle with doing the right thing. It's against human nature to do what's right. That's why it's so hard. How many times during the day do you battle against doing what's right? We don't think about that. We think about battling against doing what's wrong. It's our mission to reverse this natural tendency. We have to train ourselves to do what is against our nature. We have to establish integrity in our lives from the very start.

Things in life may not always work in the way that we want them to—we can't control that. What we *can* control is our response to what happens. Wherever we are in our lives today is due to the choices that we have made throughout our lives—ten seconds at a time—choice by choice.

Some people may be saying, "I wonder what would have happened if I had taken that job in Atlanta instead of the one in Boston?" You made that choice, and it's natural to second guess. We will be saying "What if?" for the rest of our lives. The point is—we have to make what we feel is the best choice and live with it. If it ends up being bad, then do something to change it. Just remember to learn something from the experience.

Back in the 1960s, comedian Flip Wilson used to use the catch phrase,

"The devil made me do it." It was funny, and it got laughs. But it's not true. Nobody *makes* us do anything. We choose the road we will travel—no excuses—no regrets. An excuse is a statement given for not accomplishing something. "I forgot to do it." "I'm sorry, I was too busy." "My dog ate my homework." People who have truly overcome have come to realize that excuses cannot be a part of the victory.

If a situation gets us down, we must learn to face up to it and make the best of it. I like to say, "I will do all I can possibly do, and then some." An overcomer makes a habit of working toward good decisions. They will make mistakes along the way, but the difference is they will learn to make less of them. It takes practice and the habit of getting into a routine. Proper practice makes perfect. Positive repetition breeds success—and success comes in realizing that life is not always about me—it is about all of us. To live, sometimes I have to die to my own desires. To get, I have first to be willing to give. To lead, I have to be willing to serve.

Difficulties and adversity stretch us as people. People who overcome can relate to and are more understanding of those who have pain in their lives because there is a depth in their own lives. Every person has the capacity to deal with tough situations, but it's our reaction to those hard times that shapes us. A lot depends on what foundation has been built. Going through tough times and dealing with them well is known as character-building. Change is inevitable; but we determine by our response whether we grow or not. Many times we have to learn lessons over again. I believe this is because we never learned it the first time.

I like to think of each one of us as a well. At first, when we're young and inexperienced, the well is shallow. As we get older or have to take on more difficult circumstances, the well gets deeper. As the well gets deeper, its capacity to handle more grows. If we choose not to accept responsibilities or face challenges, the well doesn't change because we have not changed.

You know people all around you who have very shallow wells. They are very shallow people. You also know people who have deep wells. They are the people who have real depth to their lives. Some people are content with being shallow. Others welcome the responsibility of having depth. Here again, there is a choice. Which type of person are you?

Experiencing the tragedy brought me to a greater love and appreciation of life. Since then I have always cherished life with a true zest. Now, my love of life is greater because I have stood at death's door. Such an experience changes you. It gives you an appreciation for the simple things in life. It gives you a new perspective on how precious and how short life really is.

Bobby Hurley, the all-American basketball player from Duke University who led the Blue Devils to two NCAA championships, was almost killed by another driver after he left the arena following a game for his professional team, the Sacramento Kings. One of the first things that Hurley talked about as he recovered from the initial surgeries was how much more he appreciated life. Life is fragile. It's brief. And it's not to be taken for granted.

Jim Valvano, the coach of the 1983 National Champion North Carolina State basketball team, died of cancer in 1993. In the winter before his death, he made an appearance at the ESPY Awards honoring excellence in athletics. Anyone who saw and heard his speech knows that it was a tremendously moving experience. Valvano, knowing that he did not have long to live, wanted to remind everyone of how precious life is and to treat it with respect. His motto that still rings in the hearts of athletes and sportscasters across the country is, "Don't give up. Don't ever give up."

Life is but a vapor. My life could have easily been taken that October night. The heartache and pain that I went through after that night allowed my personal well to become deep. I now adore every second and minute of life that I have.

Victorious people treasure life. They fall down just as many times as others, and they recognize that life will always have shortcomings and struggles—but it's how they respond that matters—their willingness to get back up. It is not easy to say the least. It hurts and we all know that. You have to climb above these things and put them under your feet. Stand on top of them and don't let them drag you down.

To live triumphantly, you want to live life to the fullest—to remember that every decision you make is of utmost importance. Enjoy the moment. For every decision you make, there will always be an outcome—whether good or bad. Practice, routine, habit, balance, and priority are important components in your life. Each decision we make takes no more than ten seconds, though the outcome could have lasting effects. Each decision either strengthens or weakens our life's foundations.

Good lifestyle choices are essential to triumphant living. Even when you make the wrong choice, it's never too late to turn your life around. It's one decision, ten seconds at a time!

CHAPTER

20

Can I Make a Difference?

People in general have problems and are looking for hope. This may not be more evident anywhere than in the lives of young people. A combination of events started me thinking that I could make a greater difference for more people, especially the younger generation. The first time I really began to understand this was that assembly program at Mineola High School on Long Island, New York, exactly one year to the day after the accident happened—and the positive response that the students and faculty gave me. The response from that program was overwhelming. From that point on, I knew that I *had* to alert young people to the dangers of drug and alcohol abuse, the importance of making good ten-second decisions, and how to work through their life's pain.

I had overcome so much adversity and difficulty to get to that point in my life that I wanted to share with as many people as possible so that they, too, could overcome anything that would stand in their way.

More and more, I would be asked to speak to various groups and share my heart. People want to know that they are not the only ones dealing with their problem—that there are others who can relate. In addition to talking about the dangers of drug and alcohol abuse, I incorporated decision making, forgiveness, and overcoming into my talks.

I have a desire and burden for youth and want to touch as many people as I can. It's very clear to me now: My experience in teaching health education, coaching football, basketball, track, and baseball, working with groups such as SADD, the Fellowship of Christian Athletes, being a family-life and sex-education instructor, a high-school guidance counselor, and my educational degrees (a B.S. in HPE and master's degree in counseling), along with overcoming the tragedy, had prepared me for this next step—motivational speaking. But if you had told me when I was growing up that I would be doing what I am today, I would have laughed in your face. Me, a speaker? As a child I would cry when I had to speak in front of others.

In September 1991 I spent several nights wrestling with the idea of pursuing speaking on a more active level. Somehow I felt the peace that this is what my life was spared for. Maybe I too could have an impact on not only the lives of young people, but people of all generations. By turning my tragedy into triumph, maybe I too, could make a difference.

When I brought this to the attention of others, I was supported wholeheartedly. Different people were instrumental in my decision to go into full-time speaking. The first, and most important person, was my wife, Suzy. I felt this was something that I might like to do, but I was sensitive to how it might affect her. Suzy dispelled all my reservations. "Bobby, you're young. You've been through a tragic situation. Look where your life is now. With the experience that you've had working with young people, I think that you'll have the possibility of really making a difference in their lives because of what you've come through. You've worked with them. You know how they think.

You can encourage them by what you say and do in working with them." Her knowing that I would be talking about Ava didn't bother her. This amazed me—how strong she is. Just read her message in the front of the book—her telling me this and letting me know that she would stand by my side was a huge confirmation that this is what I should eventually do.

The second person was my friend Cheeks. Cheeks had a bachelor's degree and a master's in communication. When I started to share with him what I wanted to do, he said, "Petro, I was there with you from the beginning. And I took you aside at the funeral parlor that day when we were viewing Ava. I told you, 'Pet, I know this is going to sound stupid—and this is the craziest time to tell you this—but I really feel that God is going to someday touch millions through this tragedy.'" He went on to say, "I've seen where you've come from—and where you are now. This is the most incredible story of overcoming tragedy that I have ever seen. You have to share it with others so that they may be encouraged, too." That was the second of three confirmations. Doors were opening for me to pursue speaking full-time.

In the fall of 1988, I began teaching and coaching at Great Bridge High School in Chesapeake, Virginia. Sharon Ivey was a fellow driver's education teacher. One day she noticed my scars and asked me what happened. After I told her my story, she encouraged me to share this with all 600 sophomore driver education students. I did it. In the fall of 1991, I returned to Great Bridge High School after working for two years as a family-life sex-education specialist throughout the city of Chesapeake. I had now taken a position as high school guidance counselor. Bob Robinson had just become the principal. He was a friend of mine and while he was still the head coach, he had hired me in 1988 as a health education teacher and assistant football coach.

Bob knew about my story and had heard me speak on several occasions. He and the counseling department at Great Bridge encouraged me to get out and share my story with other schools around the state and in our region. Bob continued to be supportive of me even though I had to miss more and more days of school because I was getting more invitations to speak. He completely understood what I was trying to do, and allowed me to miss days to fulfill a speaking schedule that was becoming more and more demanding. Bob's encouragement and flexibility and that of several other staff at Great Bridge High School was the third confirmation that this was my new direction.

When Suzy and I were on our honeymoon cruise, we met a stand-up comedian named Stu Moss. Stu was touched by my story and encouraged me to share it more and more. He even gave me ideas about using humor in the program. Finally, when I presented this idea of speaking to family and other friends, they were all supportive.

Thanks Sharon, Mesh, and Uncle Bob. Thank you, Pastor Jerry Qualls at Glad Tidings Church in Norfolk, Virginia, for your encouragement and support. You are my modern-day Pastor Greco from Brooklyn.

What I finally had to rely on was that "knowing" feeling. "I know that I know that I know that I know—that this is what I'm supposed to do."—to bring faith, hope, and love to all who are in pain.

Youth Nation

In my years of working with people, I've been continually encouraged to focus on and target the younger generation, and I'm grateful for the opportunity to try to make a difference in their lives. Youth want to feel loved, accepted, and understood. They will run to whatever and whoever helps them feel safe and valuable. They are in search of hope at all costs. They want to know they have a purpose and destiny. Their problems, like ours, stem from fear, pain, and rejection—the need to be wanted and feel they belong. Parents, your goal should be to raise your children to discover their purpose and destiny, not to please and serve you. Don't live vicariously through them. Get in their world. Find out what makes them tick. Remember the message is sacred, not the method. Do whatever it takes. Just because you don't like a certain style or form of music or dress doesn't mean that it's wrong. When I was younger, mom would always say, "I keep telling you over and over again, and you don't get it into your thick skull". When I grew older, I told my mom that I wasn't the only one with a thick skull. If you had to keep telling me over again, then maybe the way you were telling me was wrong. Maybe you needed to change your method.

My life has been dedicated to bringing a three-fold message: First, a message of faith, hope, and courage is essential. Second, a message about the dangers of all forms of abuse, knowing that all abuse has at its roots the same source. I don't want to go after the symptom. I want to go after the problem. The problem is not the abuse or addictive behavior, the problem is in their pain. People will run to whatever eases their pain. When a person commits suicide, they are not trying to kill themselves. They are killing the pain with the only method they think will work. Abusing drugs and alcohol, sexual abuse, verbal abuse, violence and bullying all come from the same source: rejection, pain, and insecurity. Abuse destroys lives, relationships, careers, and dreams. Abuse is Destructive—period. Destructive with a capital "D." People are not only hurting themselves, they are hurting others by how they are negatively responding to pain. And third, a message to help young people understand the outcomes associated with ten-second decisions. They can be positive leaders. I want to help increase their self value. The point is—whether they choose good or bad—they have control over which decision they want to make.

Young people are growing up faster and faster today. Physically, teenagers are way ahead of where they were just five years ago. Look at high school football and basketball players, for example. They're bigger, stronger, faster—overall better athletic specimens than before. Girls who are fourteen, fifteen, and sixteen years old today look as if they should be in their twenties.

Physically, they're mature, but emotionally they may not be.

There are always exceptions to the rule, but overall, young people today are being asked to grow up much too quickly. They're asked to act like adults before they're ready to handle such a requirement. Young people need guidance. They need discipline. Whether we believe it or not, they *want* discipline.

They also want to have boundaries and goals and to take on responsibility. Too many young people view life as if they have no responsibilities. Maturity and responsibility go hand in hand. Young people need rules to be established for them. What's more, they need these rules to be enforced. If we teach children to do what is right at an early age, it can set them on the proper course for the rest of their lives. On the other hand, if we do not teach children to do what is right at an early age, it can set them on a disastrous course for the rest of their lives.

It's true. Starting at a young age, children need to learn respect and obey authority. I'm constantly reminded of this fact by stories I hear in my travels across the country. One man told me about an incident involving his parents' home in western Pennsylvania. The neighborhood in which he grew up used to be a respectable middle-class area, one in which children played football in the street, whiffle ball in the alley, and basketball in the backyard.

"In the summertime, ten or twelve of us got together every night and played a chase game called 'Release the Den.' Now," he said, "twenty years later, I go back to the old neighborhood and feel like a stranger. It has an uncomfortable and lonely feeling. It bothers me because I have so many childhood memories, but now I hate to go back there at all.

"I would love to go back and see children riding bikes in the street and playing football. I would love to see children eight and nine years old playing 'super heroes' and pretending to be Superman, Batman, and Spiderman—but they don't. They're too busy throwing rocks at my parents' back window. They have nothing better to do than to throw rocks at my parents' window. Respect—that's what is lacking. We were taught never to throw rocks at someone's window, whether the house was empty or not—period."

Respect—young people need to learn it, and it's the adults who have to take the responsibility for teaching them. Sharing the truth in love—it's getting harder every year, but we must not back down and give up hope that young people are worth the effort. They unquestionably are. They want us to be real and relatable.

I want to give young people courage. I want to give them faith—faith that no matter how devastating things can be in life, no matter how dark the situation looks, no matter how difficult, and no matter how distraught they become, they can overcome it. They must overcome it. Any difficulty and adversity can be overcome.

Young people have to be taught how to establish a strong foundation. We as adults need to either reinforce and strengthen existing foundations, tear down weak or poor ones and rebuild strong ones in their place, or help those who have never had a positive foundation at all to begin building one.

Many young people today are out of control. They think that anything goes. This is the generation of "experimentation," and experimentation is becoming common in every aspect of their lives. They're experimenting with sex, with drugs, with alcohol—whatever they can try that will give them a new thrill.

Teenagers today always talk about being "bored." This is the "Entertain Me" generation. Teachers today have to be part-teacher, part-motivator, and even part-entertainer. There is something to be said about creative teaching methods, but many young people don't feel a need to learn. They'd much rather be entertained than to put forth the effort themselves to work hard in their studies.

Yet, perhaps the most alarming trend I see is youth "experimenting with power." They believe they are invincible. This is the power of life and death. Every day there are new stories of young people killing others. For what? The thrill of power—the power to take a life. This is disturbing because there seems to be less and less value placed on human life, and we are all becoming desensitized to the violence and murder that's happening all around us. Think about it. When we watch the evening news, the top stories are usually about some horrific act against people. We see this so much it doesn't shock or affect us anymore. We're used to it. We accept it.

There must be a reversal in this. Many of us have lost our sensitivity and also our compassion. We have to start feeling again. Have we hardened ourselves so much that we don't care anymore? We can't afford to think that it happened to somebody else but not to me, so I'm not going to worry about it and maybe it'll go away. Our children learn directly from us. They watch us and observe our every move. We may not think so, but they do. If we are uncaring and apathetic adults, our children are going to follow our example and be just like we are. And that is very sad, especially when we have the power to do something about it. We need to go back to square one—back to the beginning, back to instilling strong foundations in our children. We must take the initiative and be responsible in teaching our youngsters the value of respect and of having good morals. No one else will do this for us. We have to make up our minds that we will do this, and then follow the Nike Principle: "Just Do It."

I challenge every parent, teacher, educator, youth pastor, anyone who works with adolescents to take five minutes a week—five minutes is all—to talk to or spend with a youngster in a one-on-one situation. Get in their world. Don't put them on the defensive. I guarantee that it will make all the difference in the world. Young people today are longing for someone who really cares and loves them as they are—someone whom they can talk to and trust.

We are turning into an untrusting society and the results are obvious. We must reverse this because with trust comes maturity, and with maturity comes responsibility, and with responsibility comes respect. That's what we need more of from all of us at every level. But it all starts with us. We adults are leaders and role models. We've got to set the standard and then abide by it so that it becomes the rule.

I wouldn't say that all of our young people are causing problems. Most are trying to do the best with what they know. The need to be loved and accepted is essential, but they are in danger of being influenced in the wrong direction. The pressures on our young people today are far greater than they were for any past generation because they are faced with more serious issues younger in life. What high school students would have faced in past generations are now being faced by older elementary and middle school students. They lose their innocence too soon.

Think about the importance today of image. "Image is everything," say television commercials: Wear the right clothes, use the right razor, and drink the right beer. If you do these three things, you'll have a wonderful, exciting, and fulfilling life—or so they want us to believe.

Think about the casual attitudes toward sex. More and more young people are becoming sexually active at an earlier age. Elementary school children are now entering into this trend. Children are losing their innocence much too quickly. Many of them are missing out on so much of their child-hood because of the pressures put on them to grow up. Teenagers think that they are adults and are ready to make adult decisions. They, too, are being cheated out of some of the best years of their lives—years that go by too quickly and can never be recovered.

Responsibility. That's what it comes down to—responsibility. They have to know that the choices they make affect not only themselves, but many others.

Young people need to have their energy focused in a positive direction. Time after time I hear stories of a teacher, a coach, or a clergyman who took the time to invest in a young person's life. Many of the most successful leaders, business people, and athletes have the same story—that someone older than they are was willing to take the time to help establish good foun-dations in their lives—that energy, creativity, and natural ability was culti-vated and given a chance to grow and mature. This is our responsibility as adults, to take the time to encourage young people in positive directions, to teach them how to make good ten-second choices that will lead them in the right direction.

I'm a firm believer that there is good in all of us, even those who seem hardened. Everyone is reachable. I don't believe that anyone is so far gone the wrong way that they cannot come back. We have to have hope. We have to believe there is always a way—always.

I compare struggling youth to an athletic contest—an athletic contest without rules, regulations, boundaries, referees, or time clocks. Imagine the New York Giants football team playing the Buffalo Bills in the Super Bowl. It's an all-out winner-take-all game. No referees. No sidelines. No penalty flags or fifteen-yard unsportsmanlike conduct infractions. There is no forty-second clock and there are no fifteen-minute quarters. Can you imagine the confusion and hysteria that would take place? It would be total anarchy. Fans could come to the stadium and see mass chaos as they enjoyed a hot dog and soda.

This is what's happening with many of our young people today as they get more and more out of control. They have no rules to live by, no set time they have to be in, no penalties for disobedience or disrespect. When I was growing up, I would get the belt across my behind while some of my friends would get paddled with "the board of education"—a paddle that would keep them in line.

Teens are faced with many choices. "Do whatever it takes to feel good about you. The time is now. This won't affect your future". The moment becomes a lifetime as they run to whatever calms the pain, alienation, or rejection, even if this can be destructive. To them, it temporarily helps their self-worth. More focus has been placed on sex, drugs, alcohol, and violence. Sex, with the fear of the AIDS epidemic and teenage pregnancy, is on everyone's mind. It seems our education emphasis is on having safer sex. The message is: It's okay as long as you use a condom.

The proclamation of "safe sex" is a lie. There is no such thing as safe sex. Young people are not being taught abstinence. What's wrong with abstaining from sex until marriage? What's wrong with being a virgin when you get married? What's wrong with saving yourself for that person to whom you want to give the gift that you can never take back? Let's establish strong foundations. Young people will always strive to live up to the expectations that are set for them.

Television, advertising, movies, and music are all sending mixed messages. Sexual exploitation bombards our young people. Blue jeans commercials, ads for soft drinks, fragrances, cars—they all say the same thing: you'll look satisfying, sleek, and sexy if you'll only drink… or wear… or drive… That's the key.

We are constantly being "sold" that we need things—material things, pleasure for the moment. Do whatever it takes to feel good for the moment. Everyone wants to sell you the same line. There's always a new gadget, a new thingamabob, the latest thingamajig. "You have the old one—it's time for the NEW!" Young people are being taught to judge others by the size of their wallet—instead of by the integrity of their character. There is far too much emphasis on financial success and far too little on the success of being an honest, hard-working, law-abiding citizen.

Young people are being taught, "Do whatever you need to do as long as you get ahead of the next guy. If you don't do it first, he'll do it to you. It's a dog-eat-dog world out there." You know something—it is. It always has been. It always will be. But we have to step forward and have the guts to say, "It's tough out there—it's going to be a struggle—but remember your foundations, and above all, always do what's right."

Substance abuse among our young people is on the rise again. Just like sex, according to high school counselors with whom I've worked, substance abuse is now starting at a younger age. Some fifteen-year-olds are now already considered "recovering alcoholics and addicts." What's worse, parents today have even stated, "We know the kids are going to drink, so we would rather have them drink at our home." Other parents are saying, "We know kids are going to have sex. I'll let them do it in the next room. At least they're being supervised."

What kind of mentality is this? We know the kids are going to break the law, or be promiscuous, so we may as well accept it and help them do it in a controlled environment? Is that the message that we're sending our children? We're resigned to the fact that we can't control their behavior, so we'll give in to what we know is wrong, help them to do wrong, and assist them in making poor choices? Is this the parental wisdom and knowledge that we want them to pass on to their children? What happened to our "Yes" being yes and our "No" being no? People live up to expectations.

Have we lost sight of what is right and wrong? Many of us have. We who are responsible need to return to the ideals of the past, to re-impose moral standards and constraints. Schools and families need to work more closely on this. Why is it that when we talk about morals, there's a huge outcry about not mixing religion with education? It is no secret that having good morals is a strong part of being religious and having a strong faith, but good morals also means good citizenship. Good morals lead to a healthier society. Bad morals lead to social decay. Teaching the need to be responsible for one's actions is not religion-oriented. No one likes to be physically abused. No one likes to be cheated or lied to. No one likes to have things stolen from them. Teaching people to do what is right is simply moral—not religious—education.

Think of this: The heart, mind, body, and spirit of a young person is like a sponge. Whatever it soaks up, draws in, or cleans up, that's exactly what will come out when it is squeezed. If a sponge absorbs water, it won't squeeze out orange juice. If it takes in muddy water, it won't squeeze out clean water. As the saying goes: "Garbage in, garbage out. Positive in, positive out."

It's never too late to reinforce the tenets of a good foundation. With such a breakdown in families as we see today, many times schools and motivators are the only ones left to help encourage youth.

It would be nice if the family would once again become the focal point for instilling values in young people. Even though it hasn't been this way for some years, it's never too late to give people faith, to give them hope, or give them love—the love that is so desperately needed by so many youngsters. If they don't get it from us, to whom do they turn? Their peers—their friends— the streets.

Young people are searching for answers and meaning in life. They always have and always will. Where they find these answers and this meaning is partly, if not largely, our responsibility as parents and adults. Do we want someone else to raise our children? Times have changed; our parents and grandparents would have cringed at the thought of our being raised by someone else.

What's even worse today is that children are raising children. Thus we have people without maturity or parental wisdom who are teaching young-sters their ideas of what's right and what's wrong. Two wrongs don't make a right, so why should we accept or even allow this to happen? We do because many of us aren't willing to get involved. We don't want to fight. Let some-body else take the initiative—if they start it, maybe, just maybe, I'll consider joining in. What will it take for us to realize that this is not a battle but a war that we're fighting? Some experts say that it's already too late. Some say that the damage is irreversible. I say it's not.

Each of us needs to make that ten-second decision that will change a life forever. We need to say right here and now that we're going to stop thinking about it and *do* it.

Young people will strive toward the expectations that have been set. In my life, no one had to tell those 850 students from Santa Fe High School to rally around Coach Petrocelli when he was experiencing tragedy. No one had to tell them to pack out the church in the middle of a hurricane for the memo-rial service for Ava. No one had to tell them to stand in the pouring rain, with mud up to their ankles at the cemetery, to let me know how much they loved me. They knew. They did it automatically. Why? Because they were sponges who had absorbed the love that Coach Petro had for each one of them. When it was time for them to be squeezed, the love they had absorbed came out. That's all they knew to do—to give back what had saturated their hearts.

Adults need to be more in touch with young people today. We need to know where they're coming from. As a parent or educator, we need to be familiar with their likes and dislikes. By educating ourselves in what their mind-sets are, we can more effectively communicate in their language and in their world. Their sense of reality is much different than ours. What music do they listen to? Who are the people they look up to? What lingo are they using? If we understand their language, we can be a part of their growth as individuals.

I'm not saying that we should try to speak as they do or dress or act as they do. No! But we need to be current with what's happening in their lives. A big mistake would be to try to act as if we're on their level. We're not. We have to be who we are in our own generation. We dress a certain way and talk a certain way. We should never try to be something we're not. When someone is genuine and honest, you can't dispute that. People want honesty. Even if they disagree with you, they respect you for being honest. Phoniness only hurts the situation. We know when someone is being phony and when someone is being real; we can detect it. There's a mechanism inside each one of us that can sense nonverbal communication when someone is not being truthful. It's something that we just know. Young people can see right through it, too.

I personally have worked hard at keeping up with the current trends. Whether it's watching MTV and VH1 or listening to popular music stations and reading magazines that interest young people, it's all part of understanding why they think as they do. Believe me, it's work to try and stay current with what's cool today and what's not cool tomorrow, but this is what we have to do to have a greater impact on their lives. It's well worth it, but it takes work. However, the time and energy you take to research what makes them tick will pay off in the end. You'll get their respect, and that's the first step to having an effect on their lives in a positive way.

For example, one day while working as a high-school counselor, I stepped out of my office and noticed a young man leaning against the wall. He had the appearance of someone into heavy metal music. How did I know? He was wearing a "Metallica" T-shirt. The day before, I had taken the time to watch MTV and had seen a Metallica music video so that I could be more up-to-date with my students' music.

I asked him if he had seen that particular music video. He looked at me and his eyes grew so big he could probably see the whole world at one time. He said, "Mr. Petro, you listen to Metallica? You listen to heavy metal music?" I had connected. I was in his world now. A bond was formed because of a ten-second decision I had made. We could now talk, and I could find out if something was troubling him.

Young people want to know the things they are dealing with are normal for teenage years. They want respect, discipline, boundaries, and guidelines. They want to know that someone cares for them as individuals, that someone is there for them to talk to, to help them to soak up all the positives in life. They need to know that life is wonderful and rewarding, just as they need to know about responsibility and consequences. They desperately desire love and people who will spend time with them. They want to show love, but sometimes don't know how. They want to learn to offer their love in the right way. They also want their emotions to be challenged in the right way.

I want to be a positive influence of love in their lives. I want to show them respect and hope. My goal is to show them the reason why it only takes ten seconds to change a life forever. Ten seconds can make a difference.

Let's not give up on young people. They are our future and I believe in them. Most are trying to do the best with what they have or know. We can encourage them to accomplish anything that they want to, then they can truly live up to expectations because they will have the tools and the maturity to do great things. Help them build their foundations ten seconds at a time. Ten seconds can change their lives forever, good or bad.

CHAPTER

When It's All Been Said and Done

C hanging the world...10 seconds at a time is what really matters. I've been fortunate to have the opportunity to share my story of triumph over tragedy through television, radio, other media, and personal appearances. My favorite time is usually after I've spoken when I get a chance to talk with people one-on-one. When I finish a speaking engagement, the question that always comes to my mind is, "Is this all worth it?" From the responses that I've gotten, I can say a resounding, "Yes!" The response that I have had since 1991 has been amazing. As I conclude my presentations, it seems that people always ask a similar question—the same one that a young girl from a rural Ohio community asked me after I spoke at her high school: "Bobby, how can you get up in front of people and share your story? How can you do it?"

I said to her, "Has this made a difference in your thinking? Will this possibly make a difference in your life?"

Through tear-filled eyes she said, "Yes, it has. You're a real person with real scars, pain, and triumph—not just a video or someone we read about—but a *real person* we could see and talk to. Thank you for taking ten seconds to change my life." It's hard to forget the people who pour out their thanks to you. I'll never forget her face as I felt the sincerity in her voice. "That's why I do it. That's why I can get up in front of people and share my story," I told her.

Mike came to hear me speak at a YMCA on January 11, 2002. He, along with the other 500 attendees, were family members and survivors of the 9/11 tragedy at the World Trade Center. He was the first in line at the end of the program to get a book. "Bobby, I was on the phone with my wife, she worked on the eighty-third floor of the north tower, when the first plane hit. I could hear the impact. Now, I'm left with two daughters to raise without their mother. You gave me hope. You're the first person in all these months who understands how ten seconds can change a life forever. Thank you... and please keep doing what you are doing."

Recently I had two incredible responses in the state of Maryland. I had just finished speaking three times to over three thousand students. I was now in the cafeteria signing books for the students of the school. One young girl hurriedly ran up to me grabbing my arm and said, "Mr. Bobby I just jumped off the bus that will take me to the technical school. I had to tell you this. My birthday is next week and I'll be turning eighteen. I had already written my suicide note because I had planned to kill myself on my birthday. I didn't love who I was. Then you came to my school. You gave me hope and purpose. I now know that I am of value and my life is worth living. You saved my life." I still get chills thinking about it. I just stood there and was speechless (a miracle in itself).

Recently a mother e-mailed me and thanked me for giving her daughter a copy of one of my books. "My daughter heard you speak at La Plata High School. She is 16 years old and has both cerebral palsy and learning disabilities. She waited a long time to meet with you. You were kind enough to purchase one of your books for her since she didn't have the money. Your kindness and your story touched her greatly. She was ecstatic that you referred to her as "beautiful." No one ever calls her that. This child, who struggles to read, has been patiently and diligently pouring over your book for several months now. She tells me your courage has inspired her. Words cannot express my gratitude." The greatest reward is not some type of prestige or recognition. It's the lives that are touched. It's for times such as when I traveled to a college in Pennsylvania and spoke to three thousand students. At the end of the program, a female sophomore came up to talk to me. She introduced herself and said, "Bobby, you don't know me, but you have touched my life dramatically. Several years ago, while I was a senior in high school, you spoke to our student body. I was there with my closest group of friends. We were some of the biggest 'partyers' and drinkers in the school. You didn't know this until now, but after you spoke, my friends and I were really touched. You made such a strong impact on our lives that when I told my friends you were coming here to my college, they were excited and relived the time you spoke at our high school. We discussed how your message from two years ago still has a positive influence on us today."

Recently, after I completed a program at a school in Connecticut, the school's social worker approached me and immediately began to open up. She explained how her life had been devastated because of her ex-husband's cocaine habit. She said she was exhausted physically, mentally, spiritually, and financially. I could tell that she was becoming emotional. As she slowly walked away, full of tearful emotion, she said, "You've brought me something that I have needed so desperately. You have brought me hope."

I met Brad Hurdle at the end of an assembly in April 1994 at his former high school in Perquimans County, North Carolina. Brad attended the assembly because it was dedicated to his late wife, Kim Hurdle, who was killed in December 1993 by a drunk driver. Brad explained that at this time in his life, it was like being lost in a fog, but he was touched by the relatability I had with him. Little did I know that over the next months and years, Brad and I would become great friends. These are words that Brad recently sent to me to describe his experience:

My friendship with Bobby began the day I met him and has continued for over ten years. During the first years, Bobby would call to encourage and comfort me. Whenever he was near northeastern North Carolina, he would make it a point to drive to see me. My faith had gone from somewhat dormant to very confused. In Bobby, I saw a person who lived in his own "faith." I remember after several months, Bobby telling me something very important. He asked me what my faith was based on. I gave him the "deer-in-the-headlight" look. He told me his faith was based on forgiveness and that for me to find true freedom, I would have to eventually forgive the man who killed my wife, Kim. Initially, I struggled with this. Bobby told me that if I didn't forgive this man, he would not only have taken Kim from me, but would also destroy my life as well if I chose a life of anger and resentment. Anger was the one thing that gave me a sense of control. It felt right to be angry. Yet I knew deep down inside that Bobby was right—eventually anger and unforgivness would destroy me. With Bobby's help and most importantly, God's help, I did forgive the man (not condoning the wrong he did). This was instrumental with me moving on with my life. In hindsight, I see how God strategically placed Bobby in my life. He has been—and remains—a spiritual mentor to me. By crying, encouraging, and laughing with me, Bobby inspired me to share my message with thousands of people. In 1996, I moved back to my hometown and unbeknownst to me, I fell in love again with a beautiful woman named Ginger Harris. On September 19, 1998, we were married. Bobby stood beside me as a groomsman. He had to be there—without him this day would have been incomplete. Because Bobby was willing to be used by God, today I am a happily married man with a wonderful wife and two beautiful sons, Noah and Sim. As powerful as Bobby's presentation is on stage, his impact reaches down in even a more powerful way to individuals. Though Bobby and I live miles—even states—apart and we rarely see each other, when we talk on the phone we instantly connect. We immediately feel like we just saw each other yesterday. I thank God for Bobby and his willingness to be used to help others.

For me, and many others, *Triumph Over Tragedy* inspires our own "triumph over tragedy."

While speaking recently in New York, I was encouraged by a school psychologist. She wanted to introduce me to a student with whom she had been working. After I met this student in a casual manner, the psychologist and I stepped into her office. She said to me, "You have had a major impact on the life of that young boy. Recently, he got into a legal problem. While drunk, he and several other students beat up a younger, defenseless student. They beat him up so badly they sent him to the hospital. When I met with him after your program, he was in tears. He now realized, more than ever, how much his ten-second decision had changed his life and hurt this other boy. He was seeking to get comfort and help, and I guess to find forgiveness. He experienced that in your story."

I'm reminded of a young girl in Virginia who approached me at the end of an assembly at her school. This was the third assembly at this particular school in which I shared with more than two thousand students. She came running to me, weeping and sobbing. She said, "Bobby, I'm seventeen years old. Since I was fourteen, my parents have placed me in several detention homes and other foster homes because I was incorrigible. For four years I've bounced from home to home to home, leaving nothing but a path of problems in my wake. I've talked to my parents, counselors, social workers, and psychologists but, for some reason, no one has ever been able to get through to me. You are the first person to break through and to make sense to me. Everything that everyone has ever shared with me has finally hit home because of the things you've shared. I really realize how much I want to better my life."

Many times I've had the opportunity to speak at school-sponsored evening programs. I finished speaking at a rural town in North Carolina where about two hundred students, parents, teachers, and administrators were in attendance. At the end of the presentation, an older couple came up to me.

"Bobby," the older gentleman called to me from thirty feet across the auditorium. He and his wife walked slowly toward me and I could see that they were in their late sixties.

"Thank you, Bobby," he said as the tears welled up in his eyes.

"Yes. Thank you, Bobby," his wife said in a frail and cracking voice.

I looked into their teary eyes and saw a world of sadness and hurt. Just seeing the depth of the pain in their faces caused a rush of emotion inside me that I'll never forget. I can't recall ever trying so hard not to lose my composure than that night after speaking to this particular group.

"Our son was only thirty-nine years old when he was killed two years ago by a drunk driver."

It was at that moment I knew why I had become so emotional at simply seeing the hurt in their faces. Something in my heart had identified with the grief they experienced in losing their son as I had lost Ava.

"Our boy was a good boy. He never done nothin' to hurt nobody. He always went to church, had a good job, took care of his wife, and had five beautiful children," the man said before he was overcome with tears. He stepped forward and I wrapped my arms around both him and his wife. They wept openly for several minutes. I wanted to cry, but I held it inside—to this day I don't know why.

"My son and I were very close, you see—very close," he said in a choked, whispering voice. "We're a God-fearing family and we believe that there's always a reason for whatever happens to us in life. But this—this was hard for us to accept—very hard for us to accept," he said, fighting to be strong in the face of such a painful admission. "We want to thank you for coming here tonight to our little school and sharing what happened to your wife. In a strange way, we feel that there is someone else in the world who knows a little bit about how we feel."

At that instant I couldn't hold back any longer and the tears welled in my eyes. I began to sweat because the compassion and understanding I felt from that older couple was like nothing I had felt before. Here was a couple who had gone through a loss similar to mine. They knew firsthand the frustration, the anger, the helplessness, and the loneliness of losing someone so dear.

"You don't know how much you touched us," the woman said.

"Thank you, Bobby," the man repeated again. "You just don't know how much your coming here has meant to us."

I hugged and kissed them and thanked them for encouraging me that night. As they turned and walked away into the shadows of the auditorium and out into the night, I thought to myself, "You'll never know how much you've touched me, Bobby Petrocelli, here tonight."

I stood there alone in the auditorium as the janitor took down the microphone and swept up the aisle. I can still see their faces. I can still hear their voices. I can still hear the echoes—they never knew how much they touched me that night in that little school in North Carolina. This is why I do it, for the very moments like these.

Success is something we should all strive for. It's measured in different ways. Some would say that success is measured in what you have monetarily. Others would say that success is measured in the stature that you attain as an individual, an athlete, a business person, a movie star, a politician, etc. To reach a certain goal or plateau is something to strive for—but what do we do with that position once we've attained it?

To me, a successful person is one who touches others' lives in a positive way. It doesn't matter what you choose to pursue in life—being a good housewife, a janitor, winning the World Series, being the president of the United States—whatever. Is your goal to gain prestige for yourself, or to serve others?

Let me share one final story which was shared with me as a young boy and has stayed with me throughout my life:

Several people had passed from this life and were now standing in the presence of God in heaven. They stood there looking at mansion after mansion throughout heaven. Gorgeous, spectacular, breathtaking, indescribable—words could not articulate the beauty of the gold and diamonds that shimmered in the radiance of the brightness there.

As God showed each one their mansion, they came upon the most beautiful one of all. It was on a hillside and radiated with a glow of beauty around it. The first person said, "Oh, this must be the mansion of _____, the person who worked so hard to tell people about God, clothe the hungry, and feed the poor."

Everyone else agreed and whispered among themselves. God looked at them all with a smile on His face and said, "No, this is not the mansion of _____ , who served those you described, but of the one who gave of his time, his money, and his prayers so that the other person could accomplish all that was necessary to help people in need."

Serving people in love is one of the greatest gifts we can give. I believe that in saving, helping, or giving hope to one, we are helping the world. I travel and speak wherever I can—and to whomever I can—so that those who are willing to listen may know that they can also triumph. You have to choose to do it. I did—and so can you. You can make a difference. You too can triumph over any tragedy. Friend, my ultimate desire is that you find faith, hope, and love.

When my life on earth is over—when I've shared my last story, tried to motivate and inspire that last person—I want to know that my actions truly spoke louder than my words. The words that I'll desire to hear most are, "Well done, thou good and faithful servant" (Matthew 25:21).

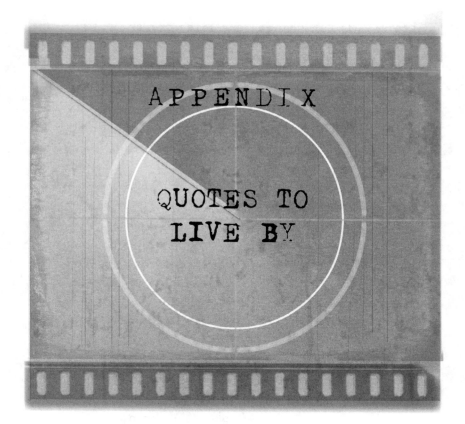

APPENDIX

QUOTES TO
LIVE BY

"You will be in a great position to have health and success if your relationship with God, your Source, is right."

—Oral Roberts

"It is impossible to accomplish anything worthwhile without the help of others."

—Unknown

"Good and Evil increase at compound interest. That is why the little decisions you and I make every day are of such infinite importance."

—C.S. Lewis

"It's not what happens to you, it's what you do about it."
                                        —W. Mitchell

"The will to win is important, but the will to prepare is vital."
                                        —Joe Paterno

"I've learned that if you keep doing what you've always done, you'll keep getting what you've always gotten."
                                        —Unknown

"No one is immune from feelings of injustice. Life's not fair, but let's not mix up life with God. God is not the source of injustice. God is fair. God is good."
                                        —Robert H. Schuller

"I have learned that success is to be measured not so much by the position that one has reached in life, as by the obstacles which he has overcome while trying to succeed."
                                        —Booker T. Washington

"Nothing splendid has ever been achieved except by those who believed that something inside of them was superior to circumstances."
                                        —Bruce Barton

"I've learned that every great achievement was once considered impossible."
                                        —Unknown

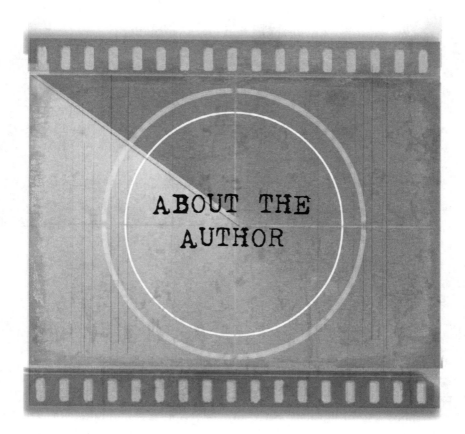

ABOUT THE
AUTHOR

Bobby Petrocelli, author, educator, and one of the most sought-after motivational speakers in the country, shares his message with people from all walks of life and every generation. He combines both his expertise and his riveting personal experience to inspire and motivate people in making the right choices in life. Bobby's life is a testimony of how one can turn pain and tragedy into triumph, hope, and victory. A drunk driver crashing through his bedroom wall, severely injuring him and instantly killing his wife, is his unforgettable story of courage, determination, and forgiveness. Recently Bobby has won the prestigious Telly Award, presented by the organization that produces the Emmy Award, for his program on overcoming obstacles.

In addition to this book, Bobby has authored and co-authored twelve different motivational books including: *Triumph Over Tragedy, 10 Seconds Is Changing Lives Forever, The Making of Unshakable Character, Unshakable Character, Lead Now—or Step Aside,* and other titles in the Teen Power Series. His story has been aired in over 100 countries and has been featured by *Geraldo, Sally Jesse Raphael, The Hour of Power, The God Squad,* The Family Channel, *Woman's World Magazine,* as well as numerous newspapers, magazines, TV and radio programs.

Bobby has been called, "The 10-Second Man." "Everything in life takes place within 10 seconds. Each decision we make, how we act, react, and respond takes no more than 10 seconds. Ten seconds can change your life forever: good or bad, right or wrong."

Bobby's zest for life and sincere love for people is communicated clearly in his message. Those who hear Bobby speak or read his authored material, always leave energized and motivated by his story and refreshed by his charismatic personality. He shares the secrets and principles of enduring faith, hope, and love in overcoming the uncontrollable tragedies that life may bring. "In life pain is inevitable; how we respond to that pain is of utmost importance."

Bobby holds a master's degree in counseling and a bachelor of science degree in health and physical education.

Bobby likes having a good time and loves people. He enjoys traveling the great outdoors—hiking, swimming, boating and other water sports. But his greatest joy is spending time with the three most important people in his life—his beautiful wife, Suzy, and their two sons, Alec and Aron.